CAMBRIDGE IGCSE® CHEMISTRY

CAMBRIDGE

Revision Guide

Chris Conoley

ACKNOWLEDGEMENTS

Cover photo © Redchanka / Shutterstock
Illustrations by Greenhill Wood Studios, Banbury, UK. Original illustrations on pages 12, 16, 20, 23, 27, 51, 55, 56, 62, 63, 82, 84, 91, 94, 97, 114 by Jouve India Private Ltd, and Anne Paganuzzi

Published by Letts Educational
An imprint of HarperCollins*Publishers*
The News Building
1 London Bridge Street
London
SE1 9GF

ISBN 978-0-00-821032-8

First published 2017

10 9 8 7 6 5 4 3 2 1

© HarperCollins*Publishers* Limited 2017
© 2017 Chris Conoley

British Library Cataloguing in Publication Data
A CIP record for this book is available from the British Library.

For my grandchildren Daniel, Oliver and Isla.

Commissioned by Katherine Wilkinson and Gillian Bowman
Project managed by Sheena Shanks
Edited by Rebecca Skinner
Proofread by Louise Robb
Cover design by Paul Oates
Typesetting by Greenhill Wood Studios, Banbury, UK
Production by Natalia Rebow and Lyndsey Rogers
Printed and bound in Great Britain by Martins the Printers

MIX
Paper from
responsible sources
FSC™ C007454

FSC
www.fsc.org

This book is produced from independently certified FSC™ paper to ensure responsible forest management.

For more information visit: www.harpercollins.co.uk/green

Contents

Chapter 3 Electrochemistry and chemical energetics

Chapter 4 Chemical reactions

Chapter 5 Acids, bases, salts and carbonates

Introduction

This revision guide will help you to prepare for your Cambridge IGCSE® Chemistry examinations. It covers all of the learning objectives in the Chemistry syllabus.

The guide is divided into eight chapters. Each chapter covers several sections of the syllabus.

The main text describes and explains the learning objectives from the Core syllabus. Supplement material is shown on a blue background. Diagrams are often used instead of, or as well as, text.

This syllabus contains many definitions, which you should learn by heart, and these are all shown in boxes with a blue outline. The definitions are summarised in the Glossary at the end of the book together with the meanings of important chemical terms.

You will find Revision tips on many of the pages in the guide. These give you hints to help you when revising. They explain how to avoid some very common errors that students make when they write answers to questions. They also point to other parts of this book where more information about a particular topic can be found.

Revision is only successful if you do something active, rather than simply reading. You could try rewriting some of the material in a different form. For example, you could convert a paragraph of text into a series of bullet points, or change a set of bullet points into a table. There are sets of Quick test questions at the end of each section, which you can use to check that you have understood and remembered the content you have just worked through. The answers to these questions are at the back of the book.

At the end of each chapter, there is a set of Exam-style practice questions. These are similar to the questions on the Cambridge theory papers. Each section has a mark allocation, which you should use to help you decide how much to write in your answer, and how much detail to give. Mark schemes for these questions are also at the back of the book. All exam-style questions and sample answers in this title were written by the author. In examinations, the way marks are awarded may be different.

You will find a list of the contents on pages 3 to 5. You could use this to keep track of your progress as you work through the guide. Perhaps you could tick the box in one colour when you have first worked through a section, and then in another colour when you have gone over it again, and have answered all of the questions correctly.

We wish you every success in your Cambridge IGCSE® Chemistry examinations and hope that this book will be really useful to you.

States of matter

There are three **states of matter** – solid, liquid and gas.

All matter is made up of particles. These particles can be atoms, molecules or ions.

The arrangement of these particles determines the structure and property of each state.

The **kinetic theory** or the **kinetic particle model of matter** is used to explain the arrangement and motion of particles in different states of matter.

> **Revision tip**
>
> **State symbols** are often used in chemical equations: (s) for solid, (l) for liquid and (g) for gas.

Solid

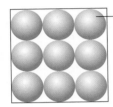 particles vibrate

- The particles are held very close together in a fixed position.
- They can only vibrate.
- They do not have enough energy to break out of position.
- Solids have a fixed volume and shape.

Liquid

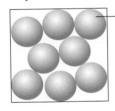 particles slide over each other and are close together

- The particles are close together.
- They can move around randomly because they have more energy.
- Liquids have a fixed volume but take up the shape of the container they are in – they can flow.

Gas

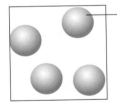 particles move quickly and are far apart

- The particles have enough energy to separate and move randomly and quite fast.
- Gases have no fixed volume and no fixed shape – they fill any container they are in and can flow.

> **Revision tip**
>
> Practise drawing particle arrangements for the three states of matter. Do not waste time drawing too many particles in an exam.

Changing state

Substances usually change state at definite temperatures.

solid $\xrightarrow{\text{heat}}$ liquid   This is **melting** and occurs at the **melting point**.

liquid $\xrightarrow{\text{heat}}$ gas   This is **boiling** and occurs at the **boiling point**.

solid $\underset{\text{cool}}{\overset{\text{heat}}{\rightleftarrows}}$ gas   This is **sublimation** and occurs at the **sublimation point**.

liquid $\xrightarrow{\text{cool}}$ solid   This is **freezing** and occurs at the **freezing point**.

gas $\xrightarrow{\text{cool}}$ liquid   This is **condensation** and occurs at the **condensation point**.

> **Revision tip**
>
> The term sublimation applies to a solid changing to gas and a gas changing to solid.

Supplement

Explaining changes of state

The kinetic theory can be used to explain changes of state.

Melting:

- Strong forces of attraction hold the particles together in a solid.
- As the temperature rises, the particles vibrate more.
- At the melting point, particles have enough energy to break free of the forces holding them in position.
- Particles can now slide over each other in the liquid state.

Boiling:

- In the liquid there are still strong forces of attraction holding the particles close together.
- As the temperature increases, the particles gain more energy and move faster. Some have enough energy to escape from the liquid surface and evaporate.
- At the boiling point, all the energy being supplied goes into breaking the forces of attraction between the particles in the liquid.
- The particles enter the gas state.
- The temperature of the liquid stays at boiling point until all the particles have gained enough energy to escape the liquid surface.

Condensing and freezing:

- These are the opposite processes to boiling and melting.
- As the temperature of a gas cools, the particles slow down.
- Forces of attraction between particles are strong enough to pull them close together and a liquid begins to form.
- As the temperature decreases further, the particles in the liquid lose more energy and move slower.
- At the freezing point, the particles no longer have enough energy to move around and the forces between them hold them in position.

> **Revision tip**
>
> **Evaporation** occurs below the boiling point, when some particles in a liquid have enough energy to escape from the liquid surface to become gas. This is different to boiling, which occurs at the boiling point, when bubbles of gas form inside the liquid and escape.

> **Revision tip**
>
> Condensation can happen above the condensation point, just like evaporation happens below the boiling point.

Pressure and temperature of gases

Pressure in a gas is caused by the particles hitting the sides of the container.

Particles in a gas move fast. Some collide with the container walls causing pressure.

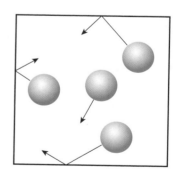

If gases are compressed into a smaller volume, there will be more particles hitting the container walls every second.

The more frequent the collisions with the container wall the higher the pressure.

Increasing the temperature makes particles move faster and increases the frequency of collisions with the container walls.

Therefore, increasing the temperature increases the pressure if the volume of the container stays constant.

Diffusion

Diffusion occurs when particles spread out and mix.

During diffusion particles move from a region of high concentration to a region of low concentration so that they become evenly mixed.

Diffusion in gases and liquids happens because their particles are in constant, random motion.

Diffusion of bromine and air
Bromine is a brown gas.

Bromine particles are heavier than air but they can diffuse into the air in the top gas jar because they move fast and randomly.

The particles in air also diffuse into the bromine in the gas jar at the bottom.

After several hours, there is no difference between the colours of the gases seen in the two gas jars.

It takes time for gases to diffuse into each other because the particles are moving randomly, so they don't all travel in the same direction. They are also constantly colliding with each other.

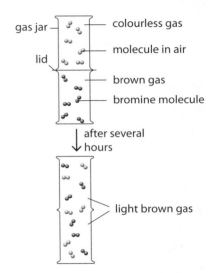

Supplement

The rate of diffusion of gases depends on the molecular mass of the gas. The heavier the molecule (particle), the slower it moves at the same temperature. This means hydrogen gas diffuses faster than any other gas.

Evidence for the kinetic particle model of matter

A **model** is what a scientist uses to explain observations.

The particles in matter cannot be seen but, when dust in a drop of liquid water is viewed under a microscope, the specks of dust are seen to be constantly moving in random directions. This is called **Brownian motion**.

A speck of dust moves randomly in water because it keeps being hit by water particles.

Supplement

Brownian motion is evidence for particles in matter. It is the particles in the liquid moving and colliding with the dust specks that makes them move. Smoke particles move in the same way because they are being hit by particles in air.

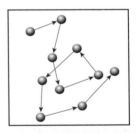
> **Revision tip**

The water particles are molecules of water, H_2O.

Quick test

1. What is the state symbol for a gas?
2. Draw the arrangement of particles in a gas.
3. Name the state of matter in which particles only vibrate and are fixed in position.
4. Give the changes of state that occur during **(a)** condensation and **(b)** sublimation.
5. Explain why pressure increases when the temperature of a gas increases if its volume remains constant.
6. If a container of air and smoke is placed under a microscope, the smoke particles are constantly moving in all directions. What name is given to this movement?

Supplement

7. Explain why smoke particles move randomly in air.

How pure?

A **mixture** is made up of more than one substance. The substances are not chemically joined, so they can usually be separated easily.

Paper chromatography

Paper **chromatography** is used to separate a mixture of coloured solids dissolved in a liquid, such as the dyes in ink or food colourings.

1. Draw a pencil baseline near the bottom of a piece of chromatography paper.
2. Put a very small spot of the liquid to be analysed on the baseline using a **capillary tube**.
   (A capillary tube is a very narrow glass tube.)
3. Stand the paper in a **solvent**, e.g. water. The pencil line must be above the solvent.
4. The solvent moves up the paper and the components in the ink move at different rates.
5. Draw a pencil line to show the height reached by the solvent.
6. Take the paper out of the solvent and leave it to dry.
7. The paper, with its separated dyes, is called a **chromatogram**.

Paper chromatography shows that this ink contains three dyes. The most soluble dye travels the furthest.

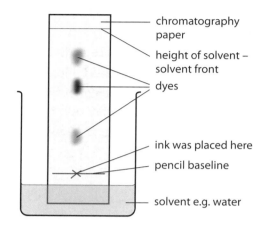

chromatography paper

height of solvent – solvent front

dyes

ink was placed here

pencil baseline

solvent e.g. water

> **Revision tip**
>
> Pencil is used to draw the baseline instead of ink because the pencil mark will not dissolve in the solvent and run up the paper.

Supplement

A chromatogram can be used to identify the components in a separated mixture.

$$R_f = \frac{\text{distance moved by substance from the baseline}}{\text{distance moved by solvent from the baseline}}$$

R_f is the **retention factor**.

The R_f value for a particular substance in a particular solvent is always the same. This means that components can be identified.

Chromatography can be used to identify colourless substances by making them visible using a **locating agent**.

Amino acids from proteins are colourless and are made visible using a locating agent (see page 140).

> **Revision tip**
>
> The distance from the baseline is usually measured to the middle of the spot.

Checking the purity of solids and liquids

Pure substances have definite melting points and boiling points that can be used to identify them.

For example, pure water melts at 0 °C. If it melts at a different temperature, it is contaminated with another substance.

Some substances in everyday life need to be pure, e.g. drugs used in medicines or substances added to food.

Methods of separating and purifying

Filtration
If a substance does not dissolve in a liquid it is **insoluble**. Insoluble solids can be removed from liquids by **filtration**, i.e. filtering through filter paper.

Evaporation
Evaporation will remove a liquid from dissolved solids. The liquid is called a **solvent**. The substance dissolved in the solvent is called a **solute**.

The liquid is heated in an evaporating basin until only solids remain.

The problem with evaporating until there is no liquid left is that all dissolved solids remain and there is still an impure substance.

Crystallisation
If there is more than one substance dissolved in a liquid, **crystallisation** may be used to separate them.

The solvent is evaporated until one of the solids is very concentrated and ready to form crystals. The hot solution is left to cool and crystals form. These crystals can then be filtered from other dissolved substances and dried.

Revision tip

To see if a substance is ready to crystallise, a glass rod is dipped into the solution and removed. If crystals form on the glass rod, the solution is at the right concentration to form crystals.

Distillation
Distillation separates a liquid from dissolved solids, i.e. it separates a solvent from its solution.

The liquid boils, turns into a vapour and is condensed back to a pure liquid in a condenser.

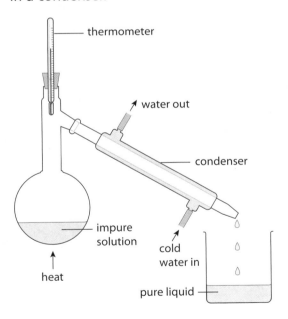

Fractional distillation
Fractional distillation separates a liquid from a mixture of two or more liquids.

The liquid mixture is heated and the liquid with the lowest boiling point vaporises first. It rises up a fractionating column and is then condensed in a condenser.

Fractional distillation is used here to separate two liquids: ethanol and water. The glass beads cool and condense the gases as they rise up the column, which aids the separation.

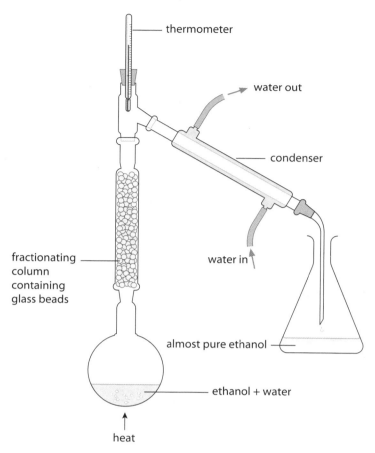

The components of petroleum are also separated using fractional distillation.

> **Revision tip**

See page 133 for more about ethanol and page 124 for more about the fractional distillation of petroleum.

Quick test

1. Name the piece of apparatus used to put a liquid sample onto chromatography paper.
2. State the name given to chromatography paper when it has the separated components on it at the end of the experiment.
3. Name the technique you could use to separate:
   (a) sand from a mixture of sand and salt solution
   (b) coloured dyes from a food colour
   (c) liquid oxygen from a mixture of liquid nitrogen and liquid oxygen
   (d) solid copper(II) sulfate from a solution of copper(II) sulfate and water.
4. Explain why a thermometer is used in the apparatus for the fractional distillation of ethanol from a mixture of ethanol and water.

Supplement

5. Calculate the R_f values of the three dyes in the paper chromatography diagram on page 10.

Elements

There are 92 **elements** found naturally on Earth and scientists have made other elements artificially.

Definition
An **element** is a substance that is made up of only one type of atom.

This means that sodium is only made up of sodium atoms and carbon is only made up of carbon atoms.

Each element has a name and a symbol.

Iron is an element made up of only iron atoms.

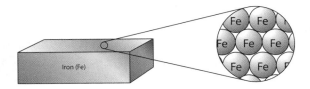

Iron (Fe)

The table shows the names and symbols of some of the elements:

Element	Symbol	Element	Symbol
aluminium	Al	lead	Pb
argon	Ar	magnesium	Mg
bromine	Br	neon	Ne
calcium	Ca	nitrogen	N
carbon	C	oxygen	O
chlorine	Cl	potassium	K
copper	Cu	silicon	Si
hydrogen	H	sodium	Na
iron	Fe	sulfur	S
iodine	I	zinc	Zn

 Revision tip

Remembering the symbols for elements that you study on your course is essential. Always write the symbol for an element in brackets when you write the name. The more you link the element name with its symbol, the easier it is to remember

Inside the atom

At the centre of the atom is its **nucleus**. It's really tiny!

The nucleus contains two different types of particle – the **proton** and **neutron**.

Most of the atom is made up of empty space with **electrons** moving around in **shells**.

Electrons have very little mass compared to the other two particles.

 Revision tip

Protons, neutrons and electrons are called sub-atomic particles. The plural of nucleus is *nuclei*.

Particle	Symbol	Relative mass	Relative charge	Location
proton	p	1	+1	in nucleus
neutron	n	1	0	in nucleus
electron	e⁻	$\frac{1}{1840}$	−1	in shells around the nucleus

The structure of a sodium atom

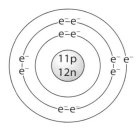

Proton number and nucleon number

<table>
<tr><td>Definitions</td></tr>
<tr><td>

Proton number (atomic number) is the number of protons in the nucleus of an atom.

Nucleon number (mass number) is the total number of protons and neutrons in the nucleus of an atom.

</td></tr>
</table>

<table>
<tr><td>▶ Revision tip</td></tr>
<tr><td>The definitions given in this book are precise and match those specified by the syllabus. The phrases should be remembered exactly.</td></tr>
</table>

The diagram of the sodium atom shows it has 11 protons. Its proton number is 11. Sodium atoms can only contain 11 protons each. If they contain a different number, they are atoms of a different element.

The sodium atom is neutral so there must be 11 negatively charged electrons ($11 \times -1 = -11$) to balance the 11 positively charged protons ($11 \times +1 = +11$).

The total number of protons and neutrons in an atom of sodium gives its nucleon number of 23 ($11 + 12 = 23$). This can be written as:

nucleon number (the number of protons + neutrons)

$^{23}_{11}\text{Na}$

proton number (the number of protons, which equals the number of electrons)

<table>
<tr><td>▶ Revision tip</td></tr>
<tr><td>You do not need to memorise proton numbers and nucleon numbers for different elements. Papers 1, 2, 3 and 4 of the exam contain a copy of the Periodic Table. This shows all the elements with their names, symbols, proton numbers and nucleon numbers. This Periodic Table is also near the end of the syllabus.</td></tr>
</table>

Isotopes

<table>
<tr><td>Definition</td></tr>
<tr><td>

Isotopes are atoms of the same element with the same proton number but a different nucleon number.

</td></tr>
</table>

Isotopes must have the same number of protons or they would not be atoms of the same element.

Isotopes also have the same number of electrons or they would not be neutral atoms.

In an isotope, it is the number of neutrons that is different.

Supplement

Isotopes have the same chemical properties because they have the same number of electrons in their outer shell (see page 16).

There are two isotopes of chlorine:

Symbol	Number of protons	Number of neutrons	Number of electrons
$^{35}_{17}Cl$	17	18	17
$^{37}_{17}Cl$	17	20	17

Isotopes can be **radioactive** or **non-radioactive**.

Radioactive isotopes are:

- atoms with unstable nuclei that emit radiation and decay into different atoms
- used in medicine to sterilise equipment and to treat cancer tumours
- used in industry to detect leaks in pipes.

Non-radioactive isotopes have atoms with stable nuclei that do not decay or emit radiation.

Quick test

1. Name the **three** sub-atomic particles that make up atoms. For each particle state its charge, relative mass and where in the atom it is found.
2. Define *proton number* and *nucleon number*.
3. A magnesium atom has a proton number of 12 and a nucleon number of 24. Show this information on the element's symbol, as in the example on page 14.
4. There are three naturally occurring isotopes of hydrogen: $^{1}_{1}H$, $^{2}_{1}H$, $^{3}_{1}H$.

   Copy out and complete a table for these isotopes using the same column headings as in the table above.
5. Explain the meaning of the term *radioactive* when it is used to describe an isotope.
6. State **one** use of radioactive isotopes in industry and **one** use in medicine.

Supplement

7. Explain why isotopes have the same chemical properties.

Arrangements of electrons in atoms

Electronic structure

Electrons are arranged in **shells** around the nucleus.

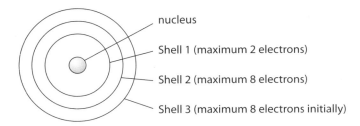

nucleus

Shell 1 (maximum 2 electrons)

Shell 2 (maximum 8 electrons)

Shell 3 (maximum 8 electrons initially)

The electrons fill up the shell closest to the nucleus first, which is Shell 1. Shell 2 fills next, then Shell 3.

This can be seen by looking at an atom of sulfur, $^{32}_{16}$S.

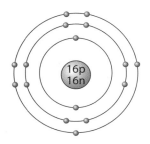

The arrangement of electrons in shells is called the **electronic structure** of an atom. This can be written as:

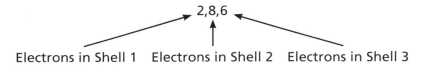

2,8,6

Electrons in Shell 1   Electrons in Shell 2   Electrons in Shell 3

The Periodic Table and electronic structure

The Periodic Table brings order to the elements:

- The elements are arranged in proton number order.
- The columns, headed by Roman numerals, show the **groups**. Elements with similar properties are grouped together.
- The group number tells you how many electrons are in the outer shell, e.g. in Group I, the outer shell of lithium, Li, sodium, Na, and potassium, K, contains 1 electron.
- Group VIII contains elements with full outer shells of electrons. These are very stable electronic structures. This group is called the **noble gase**s and they do not lose or gain electrons very easily. The importance of this is covered in the next section.
- The rows are called **periods**. In Period 1, electron Shell 1 is being filled. In Period 2, Shell 2 is being filled and in Period 3, Shell 3 is being filled.

The element symbols and electronic structures of the atoms of the first 20 elements in the Periodic Table

Groups

I	II									III	IV	V	VI	VII	VIII
			H hydrogen 1												He helium 2
Li lithium 2,1	Be beryllium 2,2									B boron 2,3	C carbon 2,4	N nitrogen 2,5	O oxygen 2,6	F fluorine 2,7	Ne neon 2,8
Na sodium 2,8,1	Mg magnesium 2,8,2									Al aluminium 2,8,3	Si silicon 2,8,4	P phosphorus 2,8,5	S sulfur 2,8,6	Cl chlorine 2,8,7	Ar argon 2,8,8
K potassium 2,8,8,1	Ca calcium 2,8,8,2														

Quick test

1. Draw the electronic structure of $^{24}_{12}$Mg.
2. State the number of the period for the element calcium.
3. Deduce the number of protons in a nitrogen atom.
4. State how many electrons are in the outer shell of Group VII elements.
5. State the number of the group that contains elements with a full outer shell of electrons.

Ions and ionic bonds

When atoms of elements react they form **compounds**.

Compounds:

- contain two or more atoms of different elements that are chemically bonded together
- have different properties from the elements that they contain.

Ionic compounds are formed when metal atoms and non-metal atoms react.

Formation of ions from atoms

Atoms are neutral because: number of protons = number of electrons.

If an atom loses electrons, there are more protons than electrons, so **positive ions** form. Metal atoms lose electrons to form positive ions.

If an atom gains electrons, there are fewer protons than electrons, so **negative ions** form. Non-metal atoms gain electrons to form negative ions.

Formation of ionic bonds in compounds

The **noble gases** of Group VIII all have stable, full outer shells.

When atoms react, they achieve this stable **noble gas electronic structure** by losing or gaining electrons to form ions.

Look at sodium chloride below. Dots and crosses are used to represent electrons.

Dot and cross diagrams for sodium and chlorine atoms showing the electron transfer

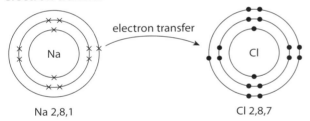

Na 2,8,1   Cl 2,8,7

Dot and cross diagrams for sodium chloride, Na⁺Cl⁻

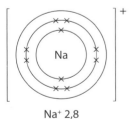   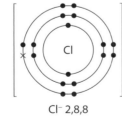

Na⁺ 2,8   Cl⁻ 2,8,8

Ions are formed by the transfer of electrons.

The oppositely charged ions are held together by a strong electrostatic attraction. This is called an **ionic bond**.

Revision tip

Some exam questions ask you to draw the outer shell of electrons only.

Definition

An **ionic bond** is the strong electrostatic attraction between oppositely charged ions.

For the Core papers 1 and 3, you only need to show the formation of ionic bonds between Group 1 metals and Group VII non-metals. Practise drawing these.

Supplement
Electron transfer from metal atoms

In Group I metals, there is only one electron to transfer from each atom. However, when magnesium (from Group II) combines with oxygen, two electrons are transferred.

Dot and cross diagram for magnesium oxide, $Mg^{2+}O^{2-}$

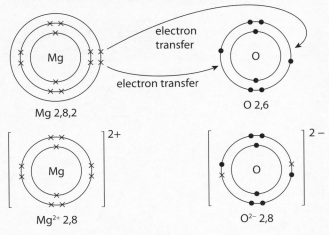

Aluminium fluoride is another ionic compound:

- Aluminium has the electronic structure 2,8,3.
- This tells you that there are three electrons in its outer shell.
- To achieve a noble gas electronic structure, these three electrons are lost to give Al^{3+}.
- Fluorine has an electronic structure 2,7.
- There are seven electrons in the outer shell.
- To achieve a noble gas electronic structure, a fluorine atom must gain one electron to form F^-.
- The formula of aluminium fluoride is AlF_3 because three F atoms are required to remove three electrons from aluminium.

Dot and cross diagram for aluminium fluoride, AlF_3

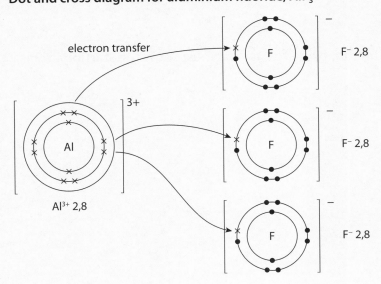

The lattice structure of ionic compounds

The electrostatic attraction between positive and negative ions is very strong, which is why ionic compounds have high melting points and boiling points.

In the solid, ions are regularly arranged in a **lattice** of alternating positive and negative ions. Ionic compounds are said to have a **giant ionic structure**.

The giant ionic lattice structure of solid sodium chloride

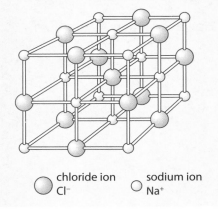

chloride ion Cl⁻   sodium ion Na⁺

Revision tip

The term *lattice* means the regular arrangement of particles, in this case ions.

Properties of ionic compounds:

* high melting points and boiling points
* low volatility (this means that the liquids do not readily evaporate)
* often soluble in water (this means that they often dissolve in water)
* do not conduct electricity when solid because the ions are fixed in the lattice
* conduct electricity when molten (liquid), or dissolved in water, because the ions are free to move (this idea is revisited on page 46 in relation to electrolysis).

Quick test

1. Explain how positive ions form.
2. Name the stable electronic arrangement that is achieved when ions form.
3. Draw dot and cross diagrams to show how potassium fluoride forms. You must show the starting atoms and the finishing ions.

Supplement

4. Draw dot and cross diagrams to show how lithium oxide forms. You must show the starting atoms and the finishing ions.
5. Describe the structure of lithium oxide.

Molecules and covalent bonds

When non-metal elements react, their atoms join together with **covalent bonds.**

Definition

A single **covalent bond** is a shared pair of electrons between two atoms.

By sharing pairs of electrons, atoms achieve a stable, full outer shell called a **noble gas configuration** (also called a **noble gas electronic structure**).

Formation of covalent bonds in molecules

The electronic structure of carbon is 2,4 and hydrogen is 1.

By sharing pairs of electrons, each atom in a molecule of methane, CH_4, achieves a noble gas configuration.

Carbon and hydrogen share pairs of electrons to form methane. A shared pair of electrons (a single covalent bond) can be shown with a single line.

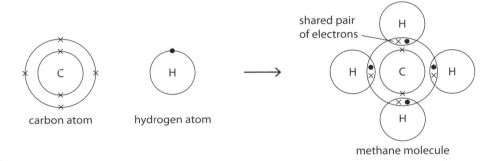

carbon atom   hydrogen atom

shared pair of electrons

methane molecule

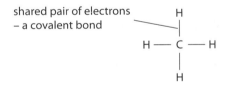

shared pair of electrons – a covalent bond

> **Revision tip**
>
> Methane is a hydrocarbon because it only contains hydrogen and carbon atoms. It is the main constituent of natural gas.

Methane is a **compound** because it contains atoms of two different elements bonded together.

Chlorine is made up diatomic molecules, Cl_2. It is an **element** because its molecules are made up of one type of atom.

By sharing a pair of electrons, each atom in a chlorine molecule achieves a noble gas configuration.

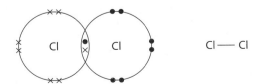

Cl — Cl

Water is made up of hydrogen and oxygen, H_2O.

Dot and cross diagram of water and its structure showing the covalent bonds

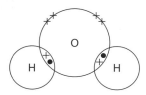

Supplement

Covalent bonding in more complex molecules

Sometimes more than one electron pair is shared to make a noble gas configuration, as in nitrogen, N_2. A nitrogen molecule has a triple bond.

Dot and cross diagrams to show the formation of a molecule of nitrogen and its structure showing the triple bond

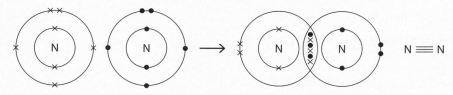

> **Revision tip**
>
> Read the questions on past papers carefully, as this will help you in the actual exam. If you are asked to draw the electronic arrangement of an atom or molecule, show all the inner shells unless the question specifically asks for the outer shell only.

Ethene, C_2H_4, has single and double bonds.

Dot and cross diagram of ethene (outer electron shells only) and its structure showing the covalent bonds

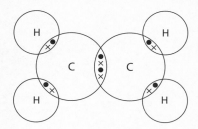

Properties of covalent compounds

Covalent bonds between atoms in simple molecules are strong. The forces between simple covalent molecules are weak. This means that their properties are very different from ionic compounds (see page 20).

Properties of covalent compounds:

- low melting points and boiling points
- high volatility (this means that the liquids readily vaporise)
- mostly insoluble in water (this means they do not dissolve in water)
- do not conduct electricity when solid or liquid because there are no charged particles, such as ions, that can move.

Supplement

Because there are only weak forces of attraction between simple covalent molecules, they can easily break free of the solid structure, so melting points are low. Particles in the liquid are only weakly held together so boiling points are also low.

Remember, in ionic compounds, melting points are high because of the strong attraction between ions.

Macromolecules

Macromolecules are **giant covalent structures** where many atoms are held together by strong covalent bonds, unlike simple covalent molecules such as chlorine and water.

Diamond and graphite

Diamond is a form of carbon in which every carbon atom is bonded to four other carbon atoms by strong covalent bonds.

Because of its giant structure and strong covalent bonds, diamond:

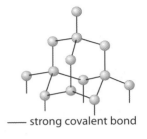

* is the hardest natural substance
* has a very high melting point
* does not conduct electricity.

—— strong covalent bond

It is used in cutting tools and drill bits.

Graphite is another form of carbon. Each carbon atom is bonded by three strong covalent bonds to make a giant structure consisting of layers of hexagons.

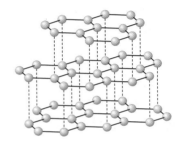

The layers can slide over each other because there are no covalent bonds between them, just weak forces of attraction between the layers. This makes graphite soft and a good lubricant.

Graphite conducts electricity because the fourth electron of every carbon atom is unbonded and moves along the layers in a **sea of delocalised electrons**.

Graphite has a high melting point because it takes a lot of heat energy to break all the carbon atoms apart to make a liquid.

Supplement

Silicon(IV) oxide, SiO_2

Silicon(IV) oxide or silicon dioxide has a structure similar to diamond, except, instead of carbon atoms, there are alternating silicon and oxygen atoms. This means it has similar properties to diamond, e.g. hard and high melting point, because all of its atoms are bonded together by strong covalent bonds.

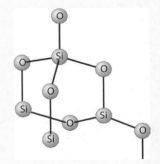

Quick test

1. Explain what is meant by a *covalent bond*.
2. Draw dot and cross diagrams for:
   (a) hydrogen, H_2
   (b) hydrogen chloride, HCl
   (c) ammonia, NH_3.
3. Explain how the structure of graphite makes it a good lubricant.

Supplement

4. Draw dot and cross diagrams for:
   (a) carbon dioxide, CO_2
   (b) methanol, CH_3OH.

Metallic bonding

Supplement

As already established, it is the bonding of the particles and the way that they are arranged that explains the properties of substances.

Metals:

- are good conductors of electricity when solid or molten (liquid)
- are **malleable** (they can be bent and hammered into shape).

These properties are explained by the structure and bonding of metals, which is called **metallic bonding**:

- The metal atoms lose one or more of their electrons to form positive ions.
- The electrons they lose go into a delocalised **sea of electrons** where they are free to move.
- The attraction between the negatively charged sea of electrons and the positively charge ions holds the metallic **lattice** together.

Revision tip

Remember, the term *lattice* means the regular arrangement of particles, in this case positive ions.

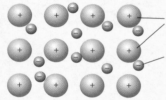

positive ions

electron in a sea of delocalised electrons

the attraction between the negatively charged sea of delocalised electrons and the positively charged ions holds the metallic lattice together

Metals conduct electricity because the electrons are free to move in the delocalised sea of electrons.

They are malleable because the metals ions are arranged in layers, which can slide over each another.

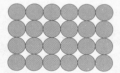

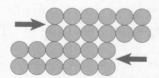

Many metals have high melting points and boiling points because of the strong attraction between the positive ions and the negative sea of electrons.

Revision tip

There is more about the properties of metals on page 91. You can read about how mixing different elements with metals to form **alloys** changes their properties on page 92.

Supplement
Quick test

1. Give the meaning of the following terms:
   (a) *malleable*
   (b) *lattice*
   (c) *delocalised sea of electrons*
2. Explain how the structure of a metal:
   (a) allows it to be malleable
   (b) makes it a good electrical conductor when solid.

1 Lakes of liquid methane exist on the surface of Titan, a moon of Saturn.

(a) Describe the arrangement and motion of methane molecules in the lakes of Titan. [2]

(b) Some of the methane escapes from the liquid surface and forms a gas.

(i) What name is given to this process? [1]

Supplement

(ii) Explain how this process occurs using the kinetic theory. [2]

(c) Describe the arrangement and motion of methane molecules in the gas state. [2]

(d) Describe what will happen to the motion of the methane molecules when the Sun warms Titan's atmosphere. [1]

(e) Solid methane also exists on Titan.

Explain why methane in this state has a fixed shape. [1]

2 The inks used in five different pens are analysed using chromatography.

The inks are labelled **A–E**.

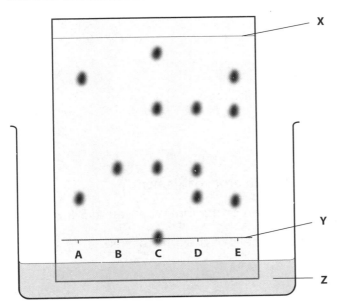

(a) To label the diagram, what should be written at points **X**, **Y** and **Z**? [3]

(b) Which ink contains only two pigments? [1]

(c) Which ink contains a pigment that is insoluble in the solvent used for this chromatography experiment? [1]

Supplement

(d) Which ink, or inks, contain a pigment with an R_f value of approximately 0.8? [1]

3 There are three naturally occurring isotopes of carbon.

(a) Complete the table to show the number of protons, neutrons and electrons in each isotope.

Atom	Number of protons	Number of neutrons	Number of electrons
$^{12}_{6}C$	6	6	6
$^{13}_{6}C$	6	7	
$^{14}_{6}C$			

[3]

(b) Define the term isotopes. [1]

(c) Explain why $^{14}_{6}C$ is radioactive, when the other two isotopes of carbon are not. [1]

Supplement

(d) Why do all three isotopes of carbon have the same chemical properties? [1]

(e) Draw the arrangement of electrons in an atom of $^{12}_{6}C$. [2]

4 The table shows the electron arrangement of the atoms of five elements.

Element	Electron structure
P	2,8,2
Q	2,8
R	2,7
S	2,1
T	2,8,8,1

(a) Which elements are in the same group of the Periodic Table? [1]

(b) Which elements are in the same period of the Periodic Table? [1]

(c) What is the proton number of Element P? [1]

(d) Which element will not form an ion? [1]

(e) Give the electronic structure of the ion formed by an atom of Element T. [1]

(f) Draw a dot and cross diagram to show the formation of the ionic compound S^+R^-.

Show the outer shells of the atoms and the outer shells of the ions formed. [2]

Supplement

5 If an element's position in the Periodic Table is known, it is possible to make predictions about its properties.

Copy the symbols and group numbers of the four elements shown to answer the questions on the next page:

- Arsenic, As (Group V)
- Iodine, I (Group VII)
- Rubidium, Rb (Group I)
- Strontium, Sr (Group II)

(a) Predict the formulae of these ionic compounds.

    (i) strontium iodide [1]

    (ii) rubidium iodide [1]

    (iii) rubidium arsenide [1]

(b) Describe the solid structure of strontium iodide.

    In your answer give the names of the particles and their positions. [2]

(c) Rubidium is a metal. In the solid state, the bonding in rubidium is called metallic bonding.

    (i) Describe what is meant by *metallic bonding*. [2]

    (ii) Explain why metallic bonding allows rubidium to be a good conductor of electricity. [2]

6 The structures of diamond and chlorine are shown.

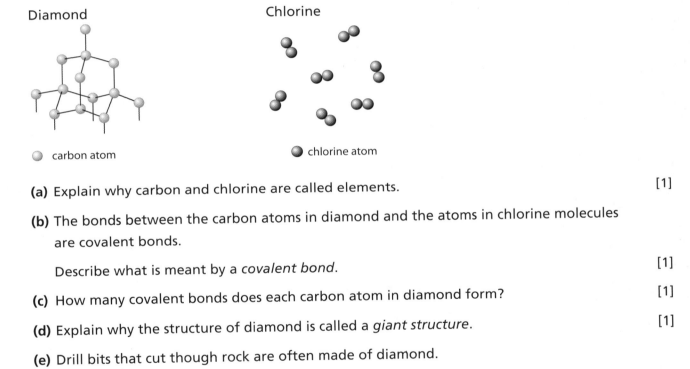

Diamond

carbon atom

Chlorine

chlorine atom

(a) Explain why carbon and chlorine are called elements. [1]

(b) The bonds between the carbon atoms in diamond and the atoms in chlorine molecules are covalent bonds.

    Describe what is meant by a *covalent bond*. [1]

(c) How many covalent bonds does each carbon atom in diamond form? [1]

(d) Explain why the structure of diamond is called a *giant structure*. [1]

(e) Drill bits that cut though rock are often made of diamond.

    (i) What property of diamond makes it suitable for drilling through rocks? [1]

    (ii) Explain how this property is related to the structure of diamond. [1]

(f) Use a dot and cross diagram to show the arrangement of electrons in a molecule of chlorine. [3]

Symbols, formulae and equations

Stoichiometry is about numbers, quantities and amounts in chemistry.

Formulae

Symbols are used to represent atoms of elements. **Formulae** are used to show that atoms have joined together in molecules or in ionic compounds.

A **formula** shows how many atoms of each element are in a molecule.

Oxygen has two atoms of oxygen per molecule, so its formula is O_2.

Some other molecules are:

- carbon dioxide, CO_2
- water, H_2O
- ammonia, NH_3
- methane, CH_4

You can work out a formula if you know the proportions of the atoms of different elements in a molecule.

A compound of nitrogen and oxygen has two atoms of oxygen for every one atom of nitrogen. Therefore, it is likely the formula is NO_2.

> **Revision tip**
>
> Formulae is the plural of formula.

Supplement

The term **molecular formula** is used to describe the formula of a molecule.

Ionic compounds do not have molecules. The formula represents the number of atoms of each element that make up the smallest complete unit.

For example:

- sodium chloride, NaCl
- sodium oxide, Na_2O.

Sometimes, you can work out a formula by looking at a diagram of an ionic lattice.

> **Revision tip**
>
> If there is only one atom of an element in a molecule, the number is not written in its formula, e.g. HCl contains one atom of H and one atom of Cl joined together.

Supplement

How to work out the formula of an ionic compound

The charges on some common ions are shown in the table below:

Positive ions		Negative ions	
Name	Charge	Name	Charge
ammonium	NH_4^+	bromide	Br^-
hydrogen	H^+	chloride	Cl^-
lithium	Li^+	hydroxide	OH^-
potassium	K^+	iodide	I^-
silver	Ag^+	nitrate	NO_3^-
sodium	Na^+		
calcium	Ca^{2+}	carbonate	CO_3^{2-}
copper(II)	Cu^{2+}	oxide	O^{2-}
iron(II)	Fe^{2+}	sulfate	SO_4^{2-}
lead(II)	Pb^{2+}	sulfide	S^{2-}
magnesium	Mg^{2+}		
zinc	Zn^{2+}		
aluminium	Al^{3+}	nitride	N^{3-}
iron(III)	Fe^{3+}	phosphate	PO_4^{3-}

Ionic compounds are neutral, so the plus and minus charges of their ions must cancel. This means you can work out their formulae:

Formula of copper(II) oxide

- the name tells you the ions present: Cu^{2+} and O^{2-}
- the charges cancel, so the formula is CuO.

Formula of potassium oxide

- ions present: K^+ and O^{2-}
- two K^+ are needed to cancel the charge on O^{2-}, so the formula is K_2O.

Formula of iron(III) nitrate

- ions present: Fe^{3+} and NO_3^-
- one Fe^{3+} is needed to cancel the charge on three NO_3^-, so the formula is $Fe(NO_3)_3$
- brackets are used around the nitrate to show that there are three nitrate ions for every one Fe^{3+}.

> ### Revision tip
>
> Try and memorise the common ions and their charges. Metals in Groups I, II and III have the same Group number as their positive charge, e.g. Na^+ because Na is in Group I. Group numbers V, VI and VII give you the number of extra electrons needed to make a full shell, so these have 3–, 2– and 1– ion charges respectively

> ### Revision tip
>
> Some metal ions have more than one charge, so the Roman numeral next to the name or symbol tells you the positive charge on the ion.

Chemical equations

A chemical equation tells you what is happening in a **reaction** when **reactants** form **products**.

When magnesium reacts with oxygen, the product magnesium oxide is formed.

The **word equation** is:

$$magnesium + oxygen \rightarrow magnesium\ oxide$$

Replace the words with formulae:

$$Mg + O_2 \rightarrow MgO$$

The number of atoms of each element must be the same on both sides, so you need to balance the equation. The formulae cannot be changed:

$$2Mg + O_2 \rightarrow 2MgO$$

You may have to add **state symbols** to an equation: $2Mg(s) + O_2(g) \rightarrow 2MgO(s)$

Revision tip

In an exam, if a question asks you to write an equation, it must be a **balanced equation**.

Quick test

1. Determine how many atoms of each element are in the following:
    (a) aluminium oxide, Al_2O_3
    (b) sulfuric acid, H_2SO_4
    (c) calcium hydroxide, $Ca(OH)_2$. Hint: in **1 (c)** there are two hydroxides, shown by the bracket and subscript 2.
2. In an ionic crystal there are two chloride ions for every zinc ion. Work out the formula of zinc chloride.
3. Hydrogen, H_2, reacts with oxygen, O_2, to form water, H_2O.
   Write the word equation and work out the balanced chemical equation for this reaction.

Supplement

4. Add state symbols to the chemical equation you wrote for Question 3.
5. Use the table on page 29 to work out the formulae of the following ionic compounds:
    (a) silver iodide
    (b) aluminium sulfide
    (c) ammonium sulfate.

Relative atomic masses and relative formula masses

Relative atomic mass, A_r

Masses of atoms are very small.

The masses of atoms are compared by using their **relative atomic masses, A_r**.

The mass of the isotope ^{12}C is the standard against which the masses of all atoms are measured.

Definition

Relative atomic mass, A_r, is the average mass of naturally occurring atoms of an element on a scale where the ^{12}C atom has exactly 12 units.

The relative atomic masses of some elements are shown in the table below:

Element	Symbol	Relative atomic mass, A_r
hydrogen	H	1
carbon	C	12
oxygen	O	16
sodium	Na	23
magnesium	Mg	24
sulfur	S	32
calcium	Ca	40
copper	Cu	64

Notice that relative atomic masses have no units.

Revision tip

You do not have to memorise relative atomic masses. All the values are in the Periodic Table and Papers 1, 2, 3 and 4 of the exam contain a copy.

Relative molecular mass (relative formula mass), M_r

Definition

Relative molecular mass, M_r, is the sum of the relative atomic masses of every atom in a molecule.

Relative formula mass, M_r, is used for ionic compounds because they do not have molecules.

Worked examples

Carbon dioxide, CO_2

M_r of CO_2 $= A_r$ of C $+ (A_r$ of O $\times 2)$

$= 12 + (16 \times 2) = 44$

Sulfuric acid, H_2SO_4

M_r of H_2SO $= (A_r$ of H $\times 2) + A_r$ of S $+ (A_r$ of O $\times 4)$

$= (1 \times 2) + 32 + (16 \times 4) = 98$

Calcium hydroxide, $Ca(OH)_2$ When there is a number outside the brackets, you need to multiply all the atoms inside the brackets by that number (in this case $\times 2$).

M_r of $Ca(OH)_2$ $= A_r$ of Ca $+ [(A_r$ of O $+ A_r$ of H$) \times 2]$

$= 40 + [(16 + 1) \times 2]$

$= 40 + (17 \times 2) = 74$

Revision tip

Be consistent with these calculations. Always put the A_r of an atom first. Then multiply by the number of those atoms in the formula.

Masses from equations

The balanced equation for magnesium reacting with oxygen to form magnesium oxide can be used with formula masses to work out masses that can react together:

Balanced equation: $2Mg$ + O_2 → $2MgO$

Relative masses: $(2 \times 24) = 48$ + $(16 \times 2) = 32$ → $2 \times (24 + 16) = 80$

Mass in grams: 48 g   +   32 g   →   80 g

Revision tip

Notice that the total mass of the reactants in an equation always equals the total mass of the products.

Worked example

How many grams of Mg and O_2 are needed to make 160 g MgO?

160 g is twice the M_r of MgO $\left(\dfrac{160}{80} = 2\right)$, so all the masses in the equation need multiplying by 2.

$48 \times 2 = 96$ g of Mg + $32 \times 2 = 64$ g of O_2 → 80×2 g = 160 g of MgO

Quick test

Use the A_r values in the table on page 31 to answer these questions.

1. Calculate the M_r of ethanol, C_2H_5OH.
2. Calculate the M_r of sodium sulfate, Na_2SO_4.
3. Calculate the M_r of copper(II) hydroxide, $Cu(OH)_2$.
4. How many grams of magnesium oxide can be made from 6 g of magnesium?
5. Copper reacts with oxygen to form copper(II) oxide. The equation is: $2Cu + O_2 \rightarrow 2CuO$.

   What mass of CuO can be made from 64 g of Cu?

Supplement

When chemists use the word **amount**, they are talking about the number of particles in a substance. The unit for amount of substance is the **mole**, which is often shortened to **mol**.

Defining the mole

Definitions
One mole is the amount of substance that contains as many particles as there are atoms in exactly 12 g of carbon-12.   **One mole** of atoms of an element is the relative atomic mass in grams.   **One mole** of molecules of a compound is the relative molecular mass in grams.   The number of particles (atoms, molecules or formula units) in one mole is 6×10^{23}. This number is huge and is known as the **Avogadro constant**.

Calculating amounts in moles

$$\text{amount in moles} = \frac{\text{mass in grams}}{\text{mass of one mole (in grams)}}$$

Worked examples

Calculate the number of moles of silicon in 56 g of silicon. (A_r of Si = 28)

$$\text{amount in moles} = \frac{\text{mass in grams}}{\text{mass of one mole (in grams)}}$$

$$\text{moles of silicon} = \frac{56\,g}{28\,g} = 2\,mol$$

Calculate the number of moles of Br_2 in 40 g of bromine. (A_r of Br = 80)

mass of one mole of Br_2 (M_r in grams) = $80 \times 2 = 160\,g$

$$\text{amount in moles} = \frac{\text{mass in grams}}{\text{mass of one mole (in grams)}}$$

$$\text{moles of } Br_2 = \frac{40\,g}{160\,g} = 0.25\,mol$$

> **Revision tip**
>
> Always check what you are being asked to calculate. Here, one mole of Br_2 molecules is not the same as one mole of Br atoms.

Calculate the mass of 0.5 mol of methane, CH_4. (A_r of C = 12 and H = 1)

one mole of CH_4 (M_r in grams) = $12 + (1 \times 4) = 16\,g$

mass in grams (rearranging the formula) = amount in moles × mass of one mole (in grams)

$$= \quad 0.5\,mol \quad \times \quad 16\,g \quad = 8\,g$$

Amounts in equations

Just as equations show the number of atoms and molecules reacting together, they also show the number of moles of atoms and molecules reacting together:

Balanced equation: $2Mg(s) + O_2(g) \rightarrow 2MgO(s)$

Moles: $\quad\quad\quad\quad 2 \quad + \quad 1 \quad \rightarrow \quad 2$

The number of moles of reactants and products in a balanced equation is known as the **mole ratio**.

Worked example

Calculate the number of moles and the mass of carbon dioxide produced when 3 g carbon reacts with excess oxygen.

The term **excess** tells you that there are more moles of oxygen than are needed to react with the carbon. Carbon is the **limiting reactant**.

Step 1 Write down the balanced equation: $\qquad$ $C(s) + O_2(g) \rightarrow CO_2(g)$

Step 2 Convert the equation into amounts (moles): 1 mole of C produces 1 mole of CO_2

In this example, you do not need to know the number of moles of O_2.

Step 3 Work out the amount being used: $\qquad$ moles of C in 3 g $= \dfrac{\text{mass in grams}}{\text{mass of one mole (in grams)}}$

$$\text{moles of C} = \frac{3g}{12g} = 0.25\,\text{mol}$$

Step 4 Scale the amounts in the equation: $\qquad$ 1 mole of C produces 1 mole of CO_2

0.25 moles of C produces 0.25 moles of CO_2

moles of CO_2 produced $= 0.25\,\text{mol}$

Step 5 Convert amount (moles) into a mass $\qquad$ mass in grams = amount in moles × mass of one mole (in grams)

$0.25\,\text{mol} \times 12\,g = 3.0\,g$

mass of CO_2 produced $= 3.0\,g$

Supplement
Quick test

1. Calculate the number of moles of iron atoms in 56 g of iron.
2. Calculate the number of moles of hydrogen molecules in 1 g of hydrogen.
3. Calculate the number of moles of sodium atoms in 46 g of sodium.
4. Work out the mass of 0.5 mol of CO_2.
5. Determine the number of moles of carbon monoxide that react with 0.1 mol iron(III) oxide in this equation: $Fe_2O_3(s) + 3CO(g) \rightarrow 2Fe(s) + 3CO_2(g)$

Volumes of gases and chemical equations

Supplement

Molar gas volume

At room temperature and pressure (r.t.p.), 1 mole of any gas has a volume of $24\,dm^3$. This is called the **molar gas volume**.

Volumes of gases and the molar gas volume

If the volume of a gas is the same at a given temperature and pressure, then it contains the same number of particles (atoms or molecules).

- The unit dm stands for decimetre, which is $10\,cm$.
- A cubic decimetre (dm^3) is $10 \times 10 \times 10 = 1000\,cm^3$.
- $24\,dm^3$ is $24\,000\,cm^3$.

Worked examples

Calculate the volume of 1 mole of hydrogen gas, $H_2(g)$, at r.t.p.

Answer: 1 mole of any gas occupies $24\,dm^3$ at r.t.p., so 1 mole of $H_2(g)$ is $24\,dm^3$.

Calculate the volume of 2 moles of hydrogen chloride, $HCl(g)$, at r.t.p.

Answer: The amount of gas is 2 moles, so the volume is $2 \times 24\,dm^3 = 48\,dm^3$.

Calculate the volume at r.t.p. of 0.25 mol of methane, $CH_4(g)$, in cm^3.

Answer: The volume of 0.25 mol of $CH_4(g) = 0.25 \times 24\,000 = 6\,000\,cm^3$

Calculating volumes of gases in chemical equations

Consider the equation: $S(s) + O_2(g) \rightarrow SO_2(g)$

- This tells you that 1 mole of sulfur will produce 1 mole of sulfur dioxide.
- At r.t.p., 1 mole of $SO_2(g)$ has a volume of $24\,dm^3$.
- This means you can use equations to calculate volumes of gases.

Worked example 1

Calculate the volume of hydrogen produced when 12 g magnesium reacts with an excess of dilute hydrochloric acid, $HCl(aq)$.

Answer: The question tells you that hydrochloric acid is in excess. This means that there are more moles of $HCl(aq)$ than are required to react with the moles of magnesium in 12 g. The **limiting reactant** is magnesium.

Step 1 Write the balanced equation:

$Mg(s) + 2HCl(aq) \rightarrow MgCl_2(aq) + H_2(g)$

Step 2 Convert the equation into amounts (moles):

1 mole of Mg produces 1 mole of H_2

In this example, you do not need to know the moles of HCl and $MgCl_2$.

Step 3 Work out the amounts being used:

$$\text{moles of Mg in 12 g} = \frac{\text{mass in grams}}{\text{mass of one mole (in grams)}}$$

$$= \frac{12\,g}{24\,g} = 0.5\,mol$$

Step 4 Scale the amounts in the equation:

1 mole of Mg produces 1 mole of H_2

0.5 mol of Mg produces 0.5 mol of H_2

Step 5 Calculate the volume of gas:

1 mole of any gas occupies $24\,dm^3$ at r.t.p.

volume of 0.5 mol H_2 = 0.5 × 24 = $12\,dm^3$

Worked example 2

Calculate the volume of oxygen required to burn $600\,cm^3$ methane at r.t.p.

Step 1 Write the balanced equation:

$$CH_4(g) + 2O_2(g) \rightarrow CO_2(g) + 2H_2O(l)$$

Step 2 Convert the equation to volumes:

1 mole of CH_4 reacts with 2 moles of O_2

1 volume of CH_4 reacts with 2 volumes of O_2

Step 3 Use the simple whole number ratio of volumes to work out the actual volume used:

$600\,cm^3$ of CH_4 reacts with 2 × $600\,cm^3$ of O_2

volume of oxygen required is $1200\,cm^3$

Supplement

Quick test

1. Calculate the volume of 0.125 mol sulfur dioxide, $SO_2(g)$, at r.t.p.
2. Calculate the volume of 64 g oxygen molecules, $O_2(g)$, at r.t.p. (A_r of O = 16)
3. Explain the meaning of the term *limiting reactant*.
4. Calculate the volume of hydrogen required to react with 9 g of carbon to form methane, $CH_4(g)$, at r.t.p.

Concentrations of solutions and chemical equations

Supplement

Concentrations

When a solid dissolves in a solvent, the concentration of the solution formed can be measured in g/dm^3 or mol/dm^3.

Worked examples

2 g sodium hydroxide, NaOH, is dissolved in $500\,cm^3$ water.

Calculate the concentration of NaOH solution in g/dm^3.

$1\,dm^3 = 1000\,cm^3$, so there are $500\,cm^3 \times 2$ in $1\,dm^3$ of NaOH(aq)

concentration of NaOH(aq) = $2\,g \times 2 = 4\,g/dm^3$

Calculate the number of moles of hydrochloric acid, HCl(aq), present in $250\,cm^3$ of $1\,mol/dm^3$ solution.

number of moles of HCl in $1\,dm^3$ ($1000\,cm^3$) = 1 mol

number of moles of HCl in $250\,cm^3 = 1 \times \dfrac{250}{1000} = 0.25\,mol$

Using concentrations to calculate amounts in chemical equations

Once the concentration of a solution is known, you can work out the number of moles that are reacting in a particular volume of that solution.

Worked example

Calculate the mass of potassium sulfate that can be made when $100\,cm^3$ of $0.1\,mol/dm^3$ sulfuric acid, H_2SO_4, reacts with an excess of potassium hydroxide, KOH, solution. (A_r of K = 39, S = 32 and O = 16)

Step 1 Write the balanced equation:

$2KOH(aq) + H_2SO_4(aq) \rightarrow K_2SO_4(aq) + 2H_2O(l)$

Step 2 Convert the equation into amounts:

2 mol of KOH + 1 mol of $H_2SO_4 \rightarrow$ 1 mol of $K_2SO_4(aq)$ + 2 mol of H_2O

Step 3 Work out the amount of H_2SO_4:

number of moles of H_2SO_4 in $1000\,cm^3$ = 0.1 mol

number of moles of H_2SO_4 in $100\,cm^3 = 0.1 \times \dfrac{100}{1000} = 0.01\,mol$

Step 4 Scale the amounts in the equation:

1 mol of H_2SO_4 produces 1 mol of K_2SO_4

0.01 mol of H_2SO_4 produces 0.01 mol of K_2SO_4

Step 5 Convert the amount (moles) into a mass:

mass in grams = amount in moles × mass of one mole (in grams)

mass of 1 mol of $K_2SO_4 = (39 \times 2) + 32 + (16 \times 4) = 174\,g$

mass of potassium sulfate that can be produced = $0.01\,mol \times 174\,g$

= $1.74\,g$

Revision tip

Always show your working in calculations. There are often marks to be gained by using the correct method, even if you make a mistake in your final answer.

Quick test

1. Calculate the concentration in g/dm^3 when 12 g of ethanoic acid is dissolved in $2 dm^3$ of water.

2. Calculate the concentration in mol/dm^3 when 7.45 g of KCl is dissolved in $100 cm^3$ of water. (A_r of K = 39 and Cl = 35.5)

3. Work out the number of moles of sodium hydroxide present in $50 cm^3$ of $2 mol/dm^3$ sulfuric acid.

4. Calculate the mass of sodium hydroxide present in $500 cm^3$ of $1 mol/dm^3$ NaOH(aq). (A_r of Na = 23, O = 16 and H = 1)

5. Calculate the mass of sodium chloride, NaCl, produced when $50 cm^3$ of $2 mol/dm^3$ hydrochloric acid, HCl, reacts with an excess of sodium hydroxide. (A_r of Na = 23 and Cl = 35.5)

Methods of measurement

In the laboratory, you will use different methods to measure physical quantities, such as masses, volumes of liquids and volumes of gases.

Mass

In the laboratory, mass is measured with a balance.

Volume of liquids and solutions

Measuring cylinders are often used to measure volumes of liquids and solutions. The volumes they measure are approximate volumes.

If the volumes need to be accurately measured, then a burette or pipette is used.

A pipette will deliver an accurate volume of liquid provided it is filled to the marked line. Pipettes in school or college laboratories usually measure a volume of 25.0 cm³.

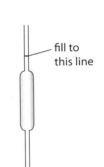

fill to this line

A burette measures different volumes accurately

Revision tip

In your exam, you may be given an experimental procedure that includes measuring the volume of a liquid using a measuring cylinder. You could then be asked to suggest an improvement to the procedure. Often the answer to this question is to use a burette or pipette because the volume of liquid measured will be more accurate.

Volumes of gases

The volume of gas produced during a reaction can be measured using a gas syringe.

This technique is often used to determine the rate of a reaction that produces a gas. The reagents are mixed and a timer is started. The volume of gas is measured at regular time intervals, often every ten seconds (see page 62).

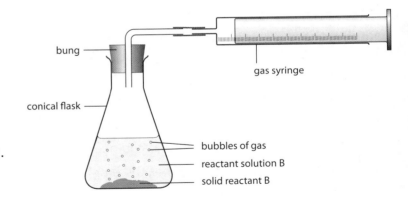

bung

gas syringe

conical flask

bubbles of gas

reactant solution B

solid reactant B

Quick test

1. Name a piece of apparatus that will accurately:
   (a) deliver 25.0 cm³ of dilute hydrochloric acid
   (b) measure 2.00 g of calcium carbonate.

2. Calcium carbonate reacts with dilute hydrochloric acid and the volume of gas produced is measured using a gas syringe. Draw and label the apparatus set-up. Label the reactants and gaseous product.

Empirical and molecular formulae

Supplement
Empirical formulae

Definition
The **empirical formula** is the simplest whole number ratio of the atoms of each element in a compound.

The empirical formula of ethane, C_2H_6, is CH_3.

If you are given the masses of each element in a compound, you can work out the empirical formula.

Sometimes you may be given the percentage composition of each element, as in the example below.

Worked example

Glucose contains carbon, hydrogen and oxygen only.

It has 40.0% carbon, 6.67% hydrogen and 53.3% oxygen by mass.

Calculate the empirical formula of glucose.

Set your answer out in columns or a table.

Revision tip

If you are given percentages of elements in a compound, imagine you have 100 g of the compound, so the percentages can become masses.

Element symbol	C	H	O
Mass in grams	40.0	6.67	53.33
Amount in moles	$\frac{40.0}{12} = 3.33$	$\frac{6.67}{1} = 6.67$	$\frac{53.33}{1} = 3.33$
Simplest ratio (divide by the smallest amount)	$\frac{3.33}{3.33} = 1$	$\frac{6.67}{3.33} = 2$	$\frac{3.33}{3.33} = 1$

The empirical formula is CH_2O.

Finding the molecular formula

The empirical formula tells you the simplest whole number ratio of different atoms in a compound. It does not tell you the actual number of atoms of each element.

The **molecular formula** tells you the actual number of atoms of each element bonded in a molecule.

Sometimes the molecular formula is the same as the empirical formula. Sometimes it is a multiple of it.

To work out the molecular formula, you need to know the relative molecular mass.

In the worked example, glucose has the empirical formula CH_2O.

This has a relative mass of $12 + (2 \times 1) + 16 = 30$.

The relative molecular mass of glucose = 180.

$\frac{180}{30} = 6$, so CH_2O must be multiplied by 6.

molecular formula of glucose = $(CH_2O) \times 6 = C_6H_{12}O_6$

Quick test

1. Work out the empirical formula for:

    (a) methane, molecular formula CH_4

    (b) ethanoic acid, molecular formula $C_2H_4O_2$.

2. Hydrazine is a compound of nitrogen and hydrogen only. It contains 87.5% nitrogen by mass.

    (a) Calculate the empirical formula of hydrazine. (A_r of N = 14 and H = 1)

    (b) Hydrazine has a relative molecular mass of 32. Deduce its molecular formula.

Percentage yield and percentage purity

Supplement

Yield

The **yield** is the mass or amount of product produced in a reaction.

The **predicted yield** is the maximum amount of a substance that is expected to be obtained if all the reactants are converted to products. This is calculated using the chemical equation.

The **actual yield** can only be found by carrying out the reaction and is the amount of a substance produced.

Percentage yield tells you how close the actual yield is to the predicted yield.

$$\text{percentage yield (\%)} = \frac{\text{actual yield}}{\text{predicted yield}} \times 100$$

It is very rare to have a 100% yield because:

- the reaction may not be finished in the time available
- material may be lost during the reaction
- unwanted by-products may be produced.

If 50 g of product is the theoretical yield from an equation and only 45 g is actually obtained, then the percentage yield can be calculated:

$$\text{percentage yield} = \frac{45}{50} \times 100 = 90\%.$$

Percentage purity

Percentage purity is used to indicate how pure a product is. This is particularly important when it comes to drugs in medicine.

$$\text{percentage purity (\%)} = \frac{\text{mass of pure substance}}{\text{mass of impure product}} \times 100$$

Supplement

Quick test

1. The predicted yield of compound Z is 40 g, but a reaction only gave 36 g. Calculate the percentage yield of compound Z.
2. In the worked example above, the predicted mass of potassium sulfate is 1.74 g. In an experiment, 1.39 g of potassium sulfate is actually made. Calculate the percentage yield.
3. A sample of 750 g of iron made in a blast furnace contains 720 g of pure iron. Calculate the percentage purity of the iron.

Exam-style practice questions

1 A cylinder of bottled gas contains butane.

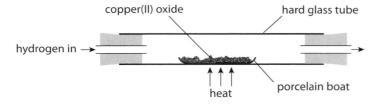

(a) Determine the molecular formula of this compound. [1]

(b) Define the term relative molecular mass. [1]

(c) Calculate the relative molecular mass of butane. (A_r of C = 12 and H = 1) [2]

(d) Propane, C_3H_8, is another bottled gas. It burns in oxygen to give carbon dioxide and water.

    (i) Write the word equation for this reaction. [1]

Supplement

    (ii) Write a balanced chemical equation for this reaction and include state symbols. [3]

2 Black copper(II) oxide is heated in a stream of hydrogen gas.

At the end of the experiment, pink, powdered copper is left in the porcelain boat.

The equation for this reaction is: $CuO(s) + H_2(g) \rightarrow Cu(s) + H_2O(l)$

(a) Calculate the relative formula mass, M_r, of copper(II) oxide. (A_r of Cu = 64 and O = 16) [1]

(b) When the reaction is complete 32 g of copper is formed.

    Calculate the mass of copper(II) oxide present at the start of the experiment. [2]

(c) Suggest why it is essential to keep hydrogen passing over the copper formed in the experiment until it is at room temperature. [2]

(d) Methane gas, CH_4, can be used in this experiment to remove oxygen from copper(II) oxide instead of hydrogen.

    Complete the chemical equation for this reaction.

    $4CuO + CH_4 \rightarrow$ ....Cu + ...H_2O + ...CO_2 [3]

Supplement

3 Sodium azide, NaN_3, explodes on heating in the following reaction:

$$2NaN_3(s) \rightarrow 2Na(s) + 3N_2(g)$$

The nitrogen produced can be used to inflate airbags in cars.

26.0 g of sodium azide is used to inflate an air bag.

(a) Calculate the number of moles of NaN_3 used. (A_r of Na = 23 and N = 14) [1]

(b) Calculate the number of moles of N_2 formed in the explosion. [1]

(c) Calculate the volume of N_2 formed in dm^3 (measured at r.t.p.). [1]

4 Explosives work by producing large numbers of gaseous molecules.

Nitroglycerine explodes as shown in this equation.

$$4C_3H_5(NO_3)_3(l) \rightarrow 12CO_2(g) + 10H_2O(g) + 6N_2(g) + O_2(g)$$

(a) Calculate the M_r of nitroglycerine. (A_r of C = 12, H = 1, N = 14 and O = 16) [2]

(b) What is meant by one mole of substance? [1]

(c) A sample of nitroglycerine produces 3 dm^3 of oxygen at r.t.p.

Calculate the total volume of gases produced during the explosion at r.t.p. [2]

(d) Calculate the mass of nitroglycerine that produces 3 dm^3 of oxygen at r.t.p. [3]

5 Vinegar is mainly a solution of aqueous ethanoic acid.

Ethanoic acid has this structure:

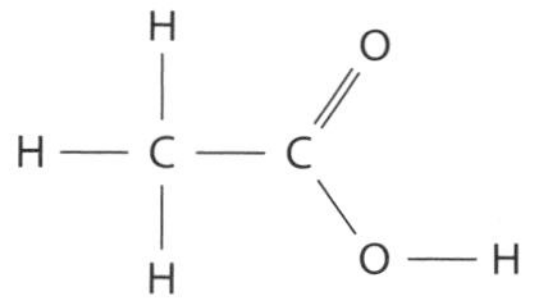

A 25.0 cm^3 sample of vinegar is analysed to find the concentration of ethanoic acid in a brand of vinegar.

(a) State the name of a piece of glassware that could be used to accurately measure 25.0 cm^3 of the vinegar. [1]

(b) Determine the molecular formula of ethanoic acid. [1]

(c) Calculate the M_r of ethanoic acid. (A_r of C = 12, H = 1 and O = 16) [2]

(d) 25.0 cm³ of vinegar is found to contain 0.020 mol of ethanoic acid.

Calculate the concentration of ethanoic acid in the vinegar in:

(i) mol/dm³   [1]   (ii) g/dm³   [1]

6 Sodium hydrogen carbonate reacts with sulfuric acid:

$$2NaHCO_3(s) + H_2SO_4(aq) \rightarrow Na_2SO_4(aq) + 2H_2O(l) + 2CO_2(g)$$

In an experiment, 50.0 cm³ of 0.200 mol/dm³ sulfuric acid was added to an excess of sodium hydrogen carbonate.

(a) Explain what is meant by the term *excess* in relation to sodium hydrogen carbonate.   [1]

(b) Calculate the number of moles of sulfuric acid used in this experiment.   [2]

(c) Deduce the number of moles of sodium hydrogen carbonate that react in this experiment.   [1]

(d) Calculate the mass of sodium hydrogen carbonate that reacts in this experiment.
(A_r of Na = 23, C = 12, H = 1 and O = 16)   [2]

(e) Suggest what mass of sodium hydrogen carbonate should be used to ensure there is an excess in this experiment.   [1]

(f) Deduce the number of moles of carbon dioxide formed from this reaction.   [1]

(g) Calculate the volume of carbon dioxide in dm³ produced in this reaction at r.t.p.   [1]

7 An oxide of nitrogen is used as an anaesthetic.

It has a percentage composition by mass: N = 64.0% and O = 36.0%.
(A_r of N = 14 and O = 16)

(a) (i) Calculate the empirical formula of the anaesthetic.   [3]

    (ii) The M_r of this compound is 44.
       Use this information to determine the molecular formula of the anaesthetic.   [1]

(b) Another oxide of nitrogen has a molecular formula N_2O_4.
Deduce its empirical formula.   [1]

8 A piece of calcium carbonate (limestone) with a mass of 15.0 g was heated in a crucible for two hours to make calcium oxide (lime).

The equation for this reaction is shown: $CaCO_3(s) \rightarrow CaO(s) + CO_2(g)$

(A_r of Ca = 40, C = 12 and O = 16)

(a) Calculate the number of moles of calcium carbonate that reacted.   [2]

(b) Predict the number of moles of calcium oxide that were made in this reaction.   [1]

(c) Calculate the mass of calcium oxide made in this reaction. This is the predicted yield.   [2]

(d) The mass of calcium oxide made in this experiment was 6.3 g.

Calculate the percentage yield of calcium oxide.   [2]

Electrolysis of molten compounds

Definition

Electrolysis is the breakdown of an ionic compound, which is molten or in aqueous solution, by the passage of electricity.

Electrolysis of molten lead(II) bromide

When ionic compounds are molten (liquid), their ions are free to move, so they can be broken down by electricity (electrolysed).

Apparatus used for the electrolysis of molten lead(II) bromide

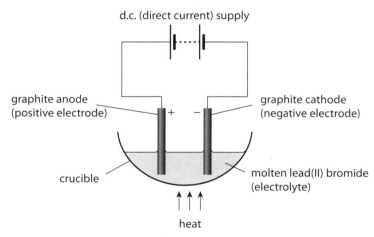

The apparatus shown above is called an **electrolysis cell**, because it is where electrolysis takes place.

The **electrolyte** is the substance that conducts electricity and gets broken down by it. Molten lead bromide is the electrolyte in this electrolysis cell.

The **electrodes** dip into the electrolyte. They are usually made of carbon (graphite), which is inert (unreactive) and has a high melting point.

The **anode** is the positive electrode and the **cathode** is the negative electrode.

During electrolysis, products are formed at the electrodes.

When molten compounds are electrolysed, metals form at the cathode(–) and non-metals form at the anode(+).

In this electrolysis cell:

- Lead is produced at the cathode(–). It is a silvery bead of molten metal.
- Bromine is produced at the anode(+). It is a brown gas.

 Revision tip

To help you remember the charge on the anode(+) and cathode(–), write the charge in brackets each time you write the words.

Lead(II) bromide is an ionic compound. When molten, its ions, Pb^{2+} and Br^-, are free to move, which is why it conducts electricity.

Pb^{2+} ions move to the cathode(–). The reaction that occurs at the cathode(–) can be shown using an **ionic half-equation**:

$$Pb^{2+} + 2e^- \rightarrow Pb$$

Pb^{2+} ions accept two electrons each to become neutral atoms. See page 29 for more information about metal ions.

When ions gain electrons, they are **reduced**.

Br^- ions move to the anode(+) and this reaction occurs:

$$2Br^- \rightarrow Br_2 + 2e^-$$

Br^- ions lose one electron each to be bromine atoms: $Br^- \rightarrow Br + e-$

Since bromine is a diatomic molecule, the bromine atoms combine:

$$2Br \rightarrow Br_2$$

When ions lose electrons, they are **oxidised**.

The transfer of charge during electrolysis

Negative ions move to the anode(+) and lose their electrons.

These electrons travel from the anode to the cathode through the conducting metal wires of the external circuit.

At the cathode(–), positive ions gain electrons.

Revision tip

To remember which ion is oxidised and which is reduced, use OIL RIG:
Oxidation Is Loss of electrons.
Reduction Is Gain of electrons.

Revision tip

Remember, it is the electrons that move in the external circuit and the ions that move in the electrolyte.

Quick test

1. Define *electrolysis*.
2. Explain the terms *anode*, *cathode* and *electrolyte*.
3. Predict the product at the anode and the product at the cathode when molten zinc chloride is electrolysed.
4. During the electrolysis of molten lead(II) bromide, what is observed at the anode?

5. Write the ionic half-equations for the formation of lead and bromine during the electrolysis of molten lead(II) bromide.
6. Explain why reduction takes place at the cathode.

Extracting aluminium using electrolysis

An **ore** is rock containing a high proportion of metal or metal compound.

Aluminium is a reactive metal that can only be extracted from its ore, bauxite, by electrolysis:

- The impurities in the ore are removed to leave pure aluminium oxide, Al_2O_3.
- The aluminium oxide must be molten to be broken down by electricity.

You can predict the products of electrolysis:

- Aluminium is a metal and will form at the cathode(−).
- Oxygen is a non-metal and will form at the anode(+).

Revision tip

You can read more about the extraction of metals and the reactivity series on page 102.

Supplement

The electrolysis cell for the industrial extraction of aluminium

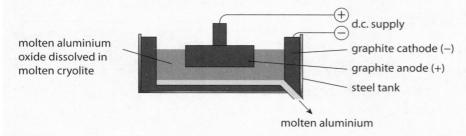

molten aluminium oxide dissolved in molten cryolite — d.c. supply — graphite cathode (−) — graphite anode (+) — steel tank — molten aluminium

Aluminium oxide has a very high melting point of over 2000 °C. This is lowered considerably, to around 1000 °C, by dissolving it in molten cryolite. This saves a lot of energy in getting Al_2O_3 molten.

The electrodes are made of graphite. In one cell, there are usually several graphite (carbon) anodes.

At the cathode(−) molten aluminium is formed: $Al^{3+} + 3e^- \rightarrow Al$

At the anode(+) oxygen gas is formed: $2O^{2-} \rightarrow O_2 + 4e^-$

The oxygen reacts with the graphite (carbon) anode to form carbon dioxide. Therefore, the anodes burn away and need to be replaced regularly.

Uses of aluminium

The properties of aluminium determine its uses:

- Aluminium is used in the manufacture of aircraft. It has a low density so, for its size, it is lightweight. It is also strong and can be made stronger by mixing it with other metals to form **alloys**.
- It is used in food containers because it is resistant to corrosion.
- It is used in overhead electric cables because it is a good conductor and has a low density, which means it won't stretch and break under its own weight. The cables usually have a steel core to strengthen them.

Revision tip

An alloy is a mixture of a metal and at least one other element. You can read more about why alloys are stronger than pure metals on page 92.

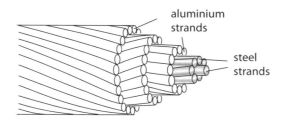

aluminium strands — steel strands

Supplement

Aluminium is a reactive metal. It does not corrode because a layer of aluminium oxide forms on its surface, which makes it appear unreactive.

Recycling aluminium

Aluminium is extensively recycled because:

- it takes a lot of energy to produce aluminium, so it is expensive to manufacture
- recycling aluminium uses only 5% of the energy it takes to produce aluminium from its ore, so it is much cheaper to recycle
- since less energy is required, less carbon dioxide is formed when **fossil fuels** are burned.

The disadvantages of recycling aluminium are:

- it has to be separated from other waste
- recycled aluminium contains impurities and this can affect its properties.

Quick test

1. Name the ore of aluminium and the aluminium compound that is concentrated in it.
2. State the products that form at the anode and cathode during the electrolysis of aluminium oxide.
3. Explain why aluminium is used to manufacture aeroplanes.
4. Explain why it is cheaper to recycle aluminium than to manufacture it from its ore.

Supplement

5. Write ionic half-equations for the formation of the products at the cathode and anode during the electrolysis of aluminium oxide.
6. Explain why aluminium is resistant to corrosion even though it is a very reactive metal.

Electrolysis of solutions

When ionic compounds dissolve in water their ions are free to move so they can be broken down by electricity (electrolysed).

Electrolysis of concentrated hydrochloric acid, HCl(aq)

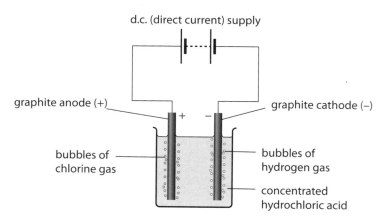

At the cathode(–) bubbles of hydrogen gas form. Hydrogen gas is colourless.

At the anode(+) bubbles of chlorine form. Chlorine is a pale green gas with a pungent smell.

Supplement

Concentrated HCl(aq) is formed by dissolving hydrogen chloride, HCl(g), in water. Although HCl is a covalent compound, it ionises in water to form $H^+(aq)$ and $Cl^-(aq)$.

Pure water is also very slightly ionised and forms $H^+(aq)$ and $OH^-(aq)$, but not enough to conduct electricity.

Reaction at the cathode(–): $2H^+ \rightarrow H_2 + 2e^-$

Reaction at anode(+): $2Cl^- \rightarrow Cl_2 + 2e^-$

Although two ions, Cl^- and OH^- move to the anode(+), Cl^- is discharged because it is more concentrated.

Electrolysis of concentrated aqueous sodium chloride, NaCl(aq)

The apparatus set-up is the same as the electrolysis cell in the previous diagram, except the electrolyte is concentrated aqueous sodium chloride.

The electrode products are the same as for concentrated HCl(aq):

- At the cathode(–) bubbles of hydrogen gas are produced.
- At the anode(+) chlorine is formed.

Supplement

The electrolysis of aqueous sodium chloride showing the movement of ions

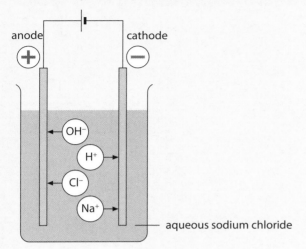

aqueous sodium chloride

Electrolysis of concentrated aqueous sodium chloride

Reaction at the cathode(–): $2H^+ \rightarrow H_2 + 2e^-$

- Na^+ ions and H^+ ions move to the cathode.
- Hydrogen is discharged because sodium is more reactive than hydrogen and remains as ions.
- The product at the cathode(–) is hydrogen gas.

Reaction at anode(+): $2Cl^- \rightarrow Cl_2 + 2e^-$

- Cl^- ions and OH^- ions move to the anode(+).
- Cl^- is discharged because it is more concentrated than OH^-.
- The product at the anode(+) is chlorine gas.

Electrolysis of dilute aqueous sodium chloride

Reaction at the cathode(–): $2H^+ \rightarrow H_2 + 2e^-$

- The product at the cathode(–) is still hydrogen gas
- Sodium ions stay in solution because they are more reactive than hydrogen ions.

Reaction at the anode(+): $4OH^- \rightarrow 2H_2O + O_2 + 4e^-$

- Cl^- ions and OH^- ions move to the anode(+).
- OH^- is discharged because it is more concentrated than Cl^-.
- The products at the anode(+) are oxygen and water.

> **Revision tip**
>
> You can predict the electrode products of other halide compounds when in dilute or concentrated aqueous solution. For example, potassium bromide solution, KBr(aq), always produces H_2 because potassium is more reactive than hydrogen. If the solution is concentrated, bromine is formed. If it is dilute, oxygen and water are released.

Manufacturing chlorine, hydrogen and sodium hydroxide using electrolysis

Concentrated aqueous sodium chloride is used to manufacture chlorine, hydrogen and sodium hydroxide:

- This solution contains Na^+, Cl^-, H^+ and OH^- ions.
- Hydrogen is produced at the cathode(–).
- Chlorine is produced at the anode(+).
- This removes H^+ and Cl^- ions from the solution.
- Na^+ and OH^- ions now form sodium hydroxide solution, NaOH(aq).
- The NaOH solution is concentrated by heating to evaporate some of the water.

Electrolysis of dilute sulfuric acid, $H_2SO_4(aq)$

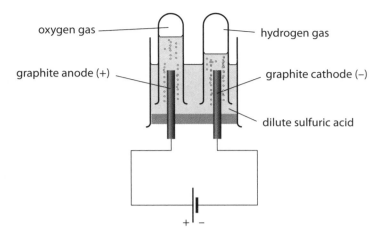

oxygen gas

hydrogen gas

graphite anode (+)

graphite cathode (−)

dilute sulfuric acid

+ −

In this electrolysis cell, the gases given off can be collected:

- At the cathode(−) hydrogen gas is produced.
- At the anode(+) oxygen gas and water are produced.

Supplement

Reaction at the cathode(−): $2H^+ \rightarrow H_2 + 2e^-$

Reaction at anode(+): $4OH^- \rightarrow 2H_2O + O_2 + 4e^-$

- SO_4^{2-} and OH^- ions move to the anode(+).
- Sulfate ions always stay in solution and hydroxide ions are discharged.

Electrolysis of aqueous copper(II) sulfate, $CuSO_4(aq)$
Using carbon (graphite) electrodes
If carbon (graphite) electrodes are used in the electrolysis cell shown on page 53, the following electrode reactions occur:

- Cathode(−): $Cu^{2+} + 2e^- \rightarrow Cu$
  Copper is deposited and brown metal coats the electrode.
- Anode(+): $4OH^- \rightarrow 2H_2O + O_2 + 4e^-$
  Although SO_4^{2-} and OH^- both move to the anode, SO_4^{2-} ions always stay in solution.

Using copper electrodes

- Cathode(−): $Cu^{2+} + 2e^- \rightarrow Cu$
  This is the same as above and copper is deposited.
- Anode(+): $Cu \rightarrow Cu^{2+} + 2e^-$
  Cu^{2+} ions go into the solution and no ions are discharged. This means the copper anode dissolves.

Purifying copper

When copper is made from its ore it is impure.

Impure copper is used for the anode and pure copper is used for the cathode. The copper(II) ions from the impure anode will transfer to the copper cathode and the pure copper cathode will increase in mass.

> **Revision tip**
>
> The copper anode dissolves, so this electrode loses mass. The cathode gains in mass as copper ions are deposited. The concentration of $Cu^{2+}(aq)$ ions in the copper(II) sulfate solution does not change. For every ion that forms copper at the cathode, another copper ion goes into solution from the anode. This means the blue colour of the solution stays the same.

Most impurities fall to the bottom of the cell but some impurities go into solution as metal ions, such as Zn^{2+}. Because these ions are very dilute, they do not discharge at the cathode.

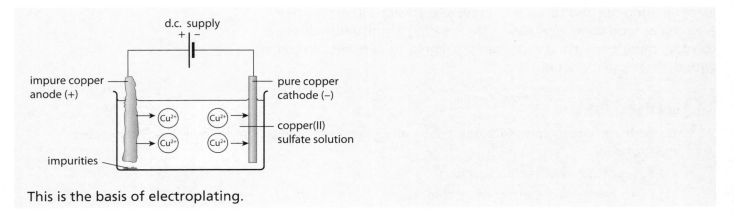

This is the basis of electroplating.

Uses of copper

Copper is a very good conductor of electricity. This is why it is used in electrical wiring.

Copper is a very good conductor of heat. It has a high melting point and it does not react with water. These properties make copper an ideal material for cooking utensils, e.g. saucepans.

> **Revision tip**
>
> The copper wires used in electric circuits in houses are coated with a layer of plastic, which is an **insulator**. This means that the plastic does not conduct electricity and the cable can be safely handled. The plastic used is also flexible and has a fairly high melting point.

> **Revision tip**
>
> You can read more about the properties of metals on page 91 and more about the low reactivity of copper on page 55.

Electroplating and its uses

Electroplating is the process of applying a thin layer of a metal to another metal using electrolysis. It can be used to add a more expensive metal to a cheaper one.

A steel teaspoon being electroplated with a layer of silver

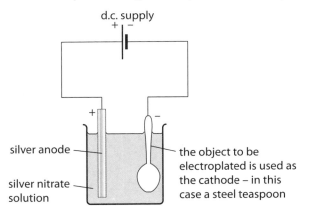

The object to be electroplated is the cathode(−).

The metal to be coated onto the object is the anode(+). In this case, silver.

The electrolyte is a solution of a **salt** of the same metal that is being used for the anode(+). In this case, silver nitrate solution $AgNO_3$(aq).

The metal ions in the solution move towards the cathode and gain electrons, e.g. $Ag^+ + e^- \rightarrow Ag$

Electroplating can also be used to prevent corrosion. Steel cans that are used as food containers have a thin coating of tin, which does not corrode, therefore air and water are prevented from coming in contact with the steel, so it does not rust.

Quick test

1. Name the products formed at the anode and the cathode when the following substances are electrolysed:

   (a) concentrated hydrochloric acid

   (b) concentrated aqueous sodium chloride

   (c) dilute sulfuric acid.

2. Steel food cans are electroplated with tin.

   (a) State what will be used for the anode and cathode in this process.

   (b) Explain how the layer of tin protects the steel can from rusting.

Supplement

3. Give the electrode reactions for the electrolysis of:

   (a) concentrated aqueous sodium chloride

   (b) dilute aqueous sodium chloride.

4. Predict the products that are formed at the anode and cathode during the electrolysis of:

   (a) dilute aqueous lithium iodide

   (b) concentrated aqueous lithium iodide.

5. Draw a diagram of the electrolysis cell used to purify copper. Give the relevant ionic half-equations.

Supplement

The **reactivity series** places metals in order of their reactivity. You can read more about the reactivity series on page 99.

The more reactive a metal, the easier it loses electrons.

When two metals of different reactivity are dipped into an electrolyte, they produce electrical energy and an electric current flows through the wire connecting them. This arrangement is called a simple **cell**.

A cell converts chemical energy into electrical energy.

Potassium	K
Sodium	Na
Calcium	Ca
Magnesium	Mg
Aluminium	Al
(Carbon	C)
Zinc	Zn
Iron	Fe
(Hydrogen	H)
Copper	Cu

increasing reactivity

A simple cell with zinc and copper electrodes

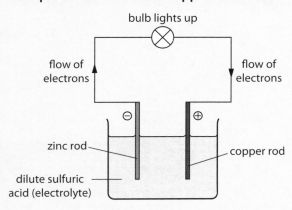

In the cell above, zinc is more reactive than copper:

- Zinc loses electrons so it is oxidised: $Zn \rightarrow Zn^{2+} + 2e^-$
- These electrons travel through the wire to the copper electrode.
- The zinc ions go into the solution.
- Zinc is the negative pole of the cell.
- Copper gains electrons so it is reduced: $Cu^{2+} + 2e^- \rightarrow Cu$
- Copper is the positive pole of the cell.

The greater the difference in reactivity of the two metals, the higher the voltage of the cell.

The voltage can be measured using a voltmeter, which is used in place of the bulb in the diagram.

Supplement
Quick test

1. Use the reactivity series to work out which pair of electrodes produces the highest voltage:

    A magnesium and zinc

    B iron and zinc

    C iron and magnesium

    D copper and magnesium

2. Explain which metal is oxidised and which is reduced when magnesium and zinc electrodes are used in a simple cell. Include in your answer ionic half-equations for the reactions occurring at the electrodes.

Chemical energetics

All chemical reactions involve energy changes.

In an **exothermic reaction**:

- energy is given out as reactants form products
- the temperature of the surroundings rises.

In an **endothermic reaction**:

- energy is taken in from the surroundings as reactants form products
- the temperature of the surroundings falls.

Temperature changes are measured with a thermometer.

Energy level diagrams

Exothermic and endothermic reactions can be shown using energy level diagrams.

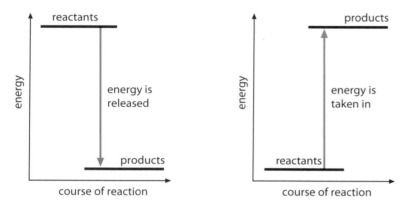

In exothermic reactions, the reactants have more energy than the products. The downward arrow shows that energy is given out during the reaction.

In endothermic reactions, the products have more energy than the reactants. The upward arrow shows that energy is taken in.

Supplement
Breaking and making bonds explains energy changes in reactions

When reactions happen, bonds in reactants break and bonds in products form:

- Bond breaking is an endothermic process.
- Bond making is an exothermic process.

Definition
Bond energy is the amount of energy needed to break one mole of a particular bond.

Bond energies can be used to calculate the energy change in a reaction.

Revision tip

Energy **ex**its in **ex**othermic reactions.
Energy **en**ters in **en**dothermic reactions.

Revision tip

In your exam, you may be asked to draw energy level diagrams from data. You will probably be given the equation for a reaction and told that energy is given out or taken in. You put this information into the appropriate energy level diagram. The arrow should always point to the product energy level and be labelled with the energy value (usually in kJ/mol).

Revision tip

Use this phrase to help you remember: **Bendo Mexo**.
Breaking (bonds) is **endo**thermic.
Making (bonds) is **exo**thermic.

The table below shows some bond energies:

Bond	Br–Br	C–H	C=O	H–Br	H–H	H–O	O=O
Bond energy (kJ/mol)	193	410	740	366	436	460	496

Worked example

Calculate the energy change for the reaction: $2H_2 + O_2 \rightarrow 2H_2O$

Step 1 Write out all the atoms and bonds in the equation:

$2H–H + O=O \rightarrow 2H–O–H$

Step 2 Energy in (bonds broken) = $(2 \times 436) + 496 = 1368\,kJ/mol$

Step 3 Energy out (bonds made) = $4 \times 460 = 1840\,kJ/mol$
(each H–O–H has two H–O)

Step 4 Energy change = energy in – energy out
$= 1368 – 1840 = –472\,kJ/mol$

Energy change is negative because energy is given out, so it is an exothermic reaction.

Revision tip

Notice that the energy released by making bonds is greater than the energy taken in by breaking bonds, so energy is given out. This makes it an exothermic reaction.

Quick test

1. Explain what is meant by an *exothermic reaction*.
2. Why does the temperature drop in an endothermic reaction?
3. Draw the energy level diagram for an endothermic reaction.

Supplement

4. **(a)** Calculate the energy change for the reaction: $H–H + Br–Br \rightarrow 2H–Br$
   (b) Explain why this is an exothermic reaction.

Fuels and energy transfer

Fuels release heat energy when they combust (burn) in oxygen. This energy can be used to do work, such as generate electricity or move a car.

Burning a fuel is an exothermic reaction.

Burning **fossil fuels** such as natural gas, which is mainly methane, produces carbon dioxide and water (see page 124 for more information about fossil fuels):

$$CH_4(g) + 2O_2(g) \rightarrow CO_2(g) + 2H_2O(l)$$

Carbon dioxide is a **greenhouse gas** linked to global warming (see page 116).

Hydrogen as a fuel

Hydrogen can be used as a fuel because it releases a lot of heat energy and it has a great advantage:

- When it combusts it only produces water: $2H_2(g) + O_2(g) \rightarrow 2H_2O(l)$
- This means it does not contribute to global warming.

However, if the hydrogen is made by burning fossil fuels, there is no environmental benefit because carbon dioxide is still produced to make it.

Radioactive isotopes as fuels

Another source of energy is from **radioactive isotopes**, such as ^{235}U, an isotope of uranium:

In nuclear power stations, ^{235}U releases large amounts of heat energy when its atoms are split. This energy is used to boil water and make steam, which generates electricity by turning turbines.

Revision tip

Hydrogen can be made by the electrolysis of concentrated aqueous sodium chloride or from the **cracking** of hydrocarbons. See page 125 for more information about cracking.

Supplement
The hydrogen fuel cell

A **fuel cell** produces electricity directly and efficiently from a chemical reaction.

In a hydrogen fuel cell, hydrogen and oxygen are pumped over electrodes and react to generate electricity. This energy can be used, for example, to power a car.

The overall reaction is $2H_2(g) + O_2(g) \rightarrow 2H_2O(l)$

Quick test

1. Explain what is mean by a *fuel*.
2. Describe an environmental benefit of using hydrogen as a fuel.
3. Explain why ^{235}U is used as a fuel.

Supplement

4. Explain what is meant by the term *fuel cell*.

Exam-style practice questions

1 This question is about the electrolysis of different substances.

(a) Complete the table.

Substance	Product at cathode	Product at anode
molten lead(II) bromide		
	calcium	chlorine
concentrated aqueous sodium chloride		chlorine
dilute sulfuric acid		

[5]

(b) The diagram shows the apparatus for the electrolysis of molten lead(II) bromide.

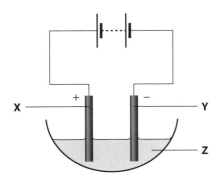

    (i) Define the term *electrolysis*. [2]

    (ii) Which label should be written at **X**, **Y** and **Z**? [1]

    (iii) Explain why the electrolysis of lead(II) bromide does not take place when it is solid. [1]

    (iv) State the name of the substance used to make the electrodes. [1]

Supplement

    (c) (i) Write ionic half-equations for the formation of calcium at the cathode and chlorine at the anode. [2]

       (ii) Which of the ionic half-equations from part (i) shows reduction?

         Explain your answer. [2]

    (d) When dilute aqueous sodium chloride is electrolysed chlorine is no longer formed at the anode.

       (i) State the name of the products formed at the anode instead of chlorine. [1]

       (ii) Write the ionic half-equation for the formation of these products. [2]

2 Aluminium is extracted from its ore by electrolysis.

    (a) What is meant by the term *ore*? [1]

    (b) State the name of the ore of aluminium. [1]

(c) State **two** uses for aluminium.

For each use, give a property of aluminium that explains why it is suitable. [4]

(d) Aluminium is one of the most recycled metals.

Give one advantage and one disadvantage of recycling aluminium. [2]

Supplement

(e) After purification, aluminium oxide from the ore is electrolysed.

(i) Name the substance into which aluminium oxide is dissolved and explain why this substance is used. [3]

(ii) Write the ionic half-equations for the reactions that occur at the anode and cathode. [2]

(iii) Explain why the anodes need to be regularly replaced. [2]

3 A student investigates the voltage produced by using different metals in a simple cell.

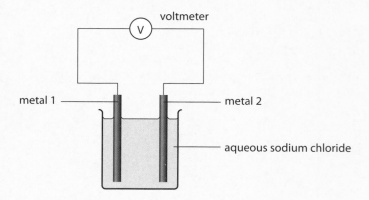

The results are recorded in the table below.

Metal 1 \ Metal 2	Voltage / V			
	copper	magnesium	tin	zinc
copper	0.0			
magnesium	1.4	0.0		
tin	0.2	1.1	0.0	
zinc	0.6	0.8	0.3	0.0

(a) Name the electrolyte used in this experiment. [1]

(b) Explain why results of 0.0 V were obtained when the same metal was used for both electrodes in the cell. [1]

(c) (i) Name the pair of metals that gave the highest cell voltage. [1]

(ii) Explain this result using ideas about the reactivity of the metals. [2]

(d) In this experiment, electrons always flow into the wire from magnesium to the voltmeter.

(i) Write the ionic half-equation for the reaction that occurs at the magnesium electrode. [1]

(ii) Use the half-equation you have written to explain the movement of electrons from magnesium into the wire. [2]

(e) Which metal, tin or zinc, is more reactive?

Give a reason for your choice. [1]

4 Methane is the main compound in natural gas.

The energy level diagram for the complete combustion of methane is shown:

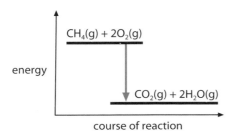

(a) State whether this reaction is exothermic or endothermic.

Explain your reasoning. [2]

(b) The structures of the reactants and products are shown:

$$H-\underset{\underset{H}{|}}{\overset{\overset{H}{|}}{C}}-H \ + \ 2O=O \ \rightarrow \ O=C=O \ + \ 2H-O-H$$

(i) What type of bonds are shown in this equation? [1]

Supplement

(ii) Which bonds are made in this reaction? [1]

(iii) Is energy released or taken in when bonds are made? [1]

5 One of the reactions that occurs in a blast furnace is shown:

$C(s) + CO_2(g) \rightarrow 2CO(g)$

(a) This reaction is endothermic.

Explain what is meant by an *endothermic reaction*. [1]

Supplement

(b) Draw the energy level diagram for this reaction. [3]

(c) Explain how the difference between bond breaking and bond making causes this reaction to be endothermic. [2]

Investigating rates of reaction

Physical and chemical changes

A chemical change happens during a reaction:

- At least one new substance is made.
- There are often observable changes, e.g. a change in colour, effervescence (bubbling) and/or a temperature change.

A physical change produces no new substances. Dissolving and changes of state are examples.

Measuring rates of reaction

Reactions can be very fast (e.g. a gas explosion) or very slow (e.g. rusting).

The **rate of reaction** can be found by measuring:

- the rate at which a reactant is used up
- the rate at which a product is formed.

Carbon dioxide gas is formed when hydrochloric acid reacts with calcium carbonate (marble chips):

$$CaCO_3(s) + 2HCl(aq) \rightarrow CaCl_2(aq) + CO_2(g) + H_2O(l)$$

The rate of reaction can be measured by recording the volume of CO_2 produced at regular time intervals.

- Add the acid to the calcium carbonate (marble chips) and quickly put the bung in.
- Start the timer immediately and measure the volume every 10 seconds.
- Plot a graph of the results (as shown in the diagram below).

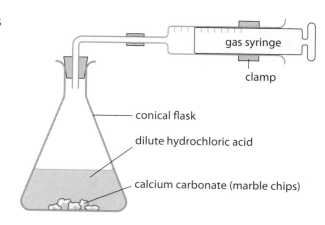

gas syringe

clamp

conical flask

dilute hydrochloric acid

calcium carbonate (marble chips)

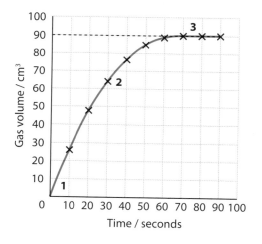

Gas volume / cm³

Time / seconds

> **Revision tip**
>
> When you draw a graph:
> - label the axes with the physical quantity and unit, e.g. time / s
> - choose a scale that uses more than half the grid in both directions.

This graph shows the rate of reaction over time. The gradient of the curve gives the rate:

- At **1**, the gradient of the graph is at its steepest showing the rate is at its highest. This is because the concentration of particles is at its highest.

- At **2**, the gradient of the curve is getting less steep, so the rate is slowing. The reactant particles are being used up, so they are less concentrated.
- At **3**, the graph has levelled out. The rate of reaction is zero because all the reactant particles have reacted.

Investigating the rate of reaction using mass loss

As the calcium carbonate reacts with hydrochloric acid, there is a loss of mass because the carbon dioxide gas escapes.

The reaction can be followed using a balance:

- As soon as the HCl(aq) is added to $CaCO_3$, record the mass and start the timer.
- Record the mass every 10 seconds until the reaction stops.
- Plot a graph of the results (as shown below).

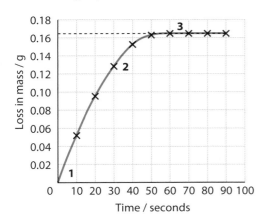

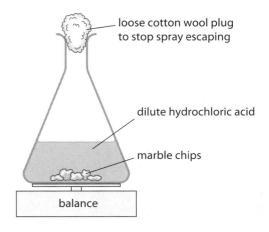

Notice that in this experiment, the vertical axis is mass loss in grams.

The shape of the graph is similar to the graph of volume against time for the reaction between $CaCO_3$(s) and HCl(aq). The numbers next to the graph have the same explanation about the rate of this reaction, as on the previous graph.

Notice that time is plotted on the x-axis because it is the **independent variable**. This is the variable for which values are chosen by the investigator. In this case, the time intervals.

The **dependent variable** is the variable that is measured for each and every change in the independent variable. In this case, the mass lost.

Quick test

1. Describe the main difference between a physical change and a chemical change.
2. Magnesium reacts with sulfuric acid to produce hydrogen gas.
   (a) Draw a diagram of the apparatus you could use to measure the volume of hydrogen produced.
   (b) Sketch a graph of the volume of hydrogen produced against time for this reaction.
   (c) Label the graph to show where the reaction rate is (i) fastest, (ii) slowing and (iii) zero.
   (d) Outline another method that can be used to measure this rate of reaction.

Factors that affect the rate of reaction

The rate of a reaction is increased by:

- increasing the concentration of a reactant in a solution – there are more reactant particles in the same volume of solution to react
- increasing the pressure when the reactants are gases – there are the same number of reactant particles in a smaller volume of gas
- increasing the temperature – the particles have more energy
- breaking solid reactants to give a smaller particle size – there is a greater surface area of the reactant exposed to other reactants (this is why fine powders, such as flour in a flour mill, can combust at an extremely fast rate and cause explosions)
- using a catalyst
- using an enzyme.

Definitions

Catalysts are substances that increase the rate of reactions but are chemically unchanged at the end.

Enzymes are biological catalysts produced by living cells to increase the rate of reactions.

Interpreting rate graphs

Two rate graphs are shown for the same reaction under different conditions. Curve **A** shows a faster rate than curve **B**.

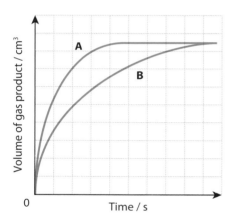

Rate curve **A** has a steeper gradient – it has a faster rate of reaction than rate curve **B** for the same reaction under different conditions.

Rate curve **A** could have been produced by:

- a higher temperature for the reaction
- a higher concentration of a reactant
- a smaller particle size for the solid reactant.

Rate curve **B** could have been produced by:

- a lower temperature for the reaction
- a lower concentration (more dilute)
- a larger particle size for the solid reactant.

Notice that both graphs level off at the same volume, so the same amount of product is produced.

Supplement

You may be asked to plan how you would investigate the effect of a particular variable on the rate of a reaction. For example, an investigation into the effect of using small marble chips compared to large marble chips on the reaction rate with hydrochloric acid.

Revision tip

A variable is something that changes during an experiment.

The **independent variable** is the size of the marble chips.

The **dependent variable** is the volume of CO_2(g) produced.

To make it a **fair test**, all other variables in the experiment must remain the same, i.e.

- the mass of the marble chips
- the concentration and volume of the HCl(aq)
- the temperature of the experiment.

These are called the **control variables**.

You could be asked to evaluate an experiment.

In this experiment, one of the major sources of error is the length of time it takes to put in the bung, because gas escapes before you can collect it in the syringe.

Quick test

1. Copy and complete these sentences.

   (a) The more concentrated a solution the .... it reacts, because there are more reactant .... in the same volume of solution.

   (b) Larger pieces of solid have a .... rate of reaction, because there is a .... surface area of reactant.

   (c) A .... increases the .... of a reaction, but is chemically .... at the end.

   (d) A .... temperature decreases the .... of ...., because the reacting particles have .... energy.

   (e) .... are biological .... produced by living .... to .... the rate of reactions.

2. Explain why food stays fresher in a cold place rather than in a warm room.

3. Small pieces of zinc react with dilute nitric acid to form hydrogen gas.

   (a) Sketch **two** graphs on the same axes for volume of hydrogen gas against time to show the effect of using two different concentrations of dilute nitric acid on the rate of reaction.

Supplement

   (b) In designing this experiment, state the **four** variables that should be kept constant.

More about rates of reaction

Supplement

Colliding particles

For a reaction to happen, reactant particles (atoms, molecules or ions) must collide with sufficient energy to react. The minimum energy required for a reaction to take place is called the **activation energy**.

Collisions between reactant particles explain why rate increases when concentration increases:

- There are more reactant particles in the same volume.
- The collision rate increases.

Collisions between reactant particles explain why rate increases when temperature increases:

- The particles move faster.
- The collision rate increases.
- The particles have more energy, so more of the colliding particles will have sufficient energy (activation energy) to react.

Revision tip

Increasing concentration only increases the collision rate. However, increasing the temperature increases the collision rate *and* increases the energy of the particles, so more particles have sufficient energy to react when they collide.

Effect of light on photochemical reactions

In **photochemical reactions**, light supplies the energy. The brighter the light, the faster the rate of reaction. This is because more particles have sufficient energy to react (activation energy).

Black and white photography

Black and white photography uses film that is coated with a silver salt. When light shines on the silver ions, Ag^+, they are reduced to silver, Ag:

$$Ag^+(s) + e^- \rightarrow Ag(s)$$

The brighter the light reflected from the subject being photographed, the darker the image. This is because silver is formed from its ions at a faster rate so, when the camera shutter is open, more silver is formed than from dimly lit subjects.

Revision tip

Remember, OIL **RIG** (page 47) – Reduction **I**s **G**ain (of electrons).

Photosynthesis

Photosynthesis is another photochemical reaction:

- Sunlight shines on the leaves of green plants.
- The light is absorbed by chlorophyll, a plant pigment.
- The energy from sunlight is used for the reaction between carbon dioxide and water to produce glucose and oxygen.

$$\text{carbon dioxide} + \text{water} \xrightarrow[\text{chlorophyll}]{\text{sunlight}} \text{glucose} + \text{oxygen}$$

Other examples of photochemical reactions are the substitution reactions of alkanes with chlorine (see page 128).

Quick test

1. Explain the effect of decreasing the temperature on the rate of a reaction in terms of collisions between particles.

2. Explain what is meant by *activation energy*.

3. An acid reacts with calcium carbonate to form carbon dioxide. Use ideas about collisions between particles to explain why decreasing the concentration of the acid decreases the reaction rate.

4. Explain why bright light increases the rate of a photochemical reaction more than dim light.

5. Give **two** examples of photochemical reactions.

Reversible reactions

Combustion reactions are examples of reactions that cannot be reversed, e.g.

methane + oxygen → carbon dioxide + water

$CH_4(g)$ + $2O_2(g)$ → $CO_2(g)$ + $2H_2O(l)$

The products cannot be reacted to make methane and oxygen again.

However, some reactions can be made to go both ways if the conditions are changed. These are called reversible reactions. This is shown in chemical equations with the symbol ⇌.

Hydrated copper(II) sulfate is blue. It can be heated to produce anhydrous copper(II) sulfate, which is white.

If water is added to anhydrous copper(II) sulfate, the colour changes from white back to blue:

$CuSO_4.5H_2O(s)$ ⇌ $CuSO_4(s)$ + $5H_2O(l)$
   blue solid   white solid

Cobalt(II) chloride can also take part in a similar reversible reaction:

$CoCl_2.6H_2O(s)$ ⇌ $CoCl_2(s)$ + $6H_2O(l)$
  pink solid   blue solid

Chemical tests for water

Both anhydrous copper(II) sulfate and anhydrous cobalt(II) chloride can be used to test if a liquid contains water (see page 112).

Add the liquid to anhydrous copper(II) sulfate, $CuSO_4$. The white powder turns blue if water is present:

$CuSO_4(s)$ + $5H_2O(l)$ ⇌ $CuSO_4.5H_2O(s)$
 white solid   blue solid

Add the liquid to anhydrous cobalt(II) chloride, $CoCl_2$. The blue colour turns pink if water is present:

$CoCl_2(s)$ + $6H_2O(l)$ ⇌ $CoCl_2.6H_2O(s)$
 blue solid   pink solid

Supplement
Reactions in equilibrium

If a reversible reaction happens in a closed container then it will reach an **equilibrium**.

At equilibrium:

- The rate of the forward reaction equals the rate of the reverse reaction.
- The amounts and concentrations of the products and reactants are constant.

> **Revision tip**
>
> The water in the formulae of hydrated crystals is shown using a dot before the H_2O, e.g. $CuSO_4.5H_2O$ and $CoCl_2.6H_2O$. *Anhydrous* means without water.

> **Revision tip**
>
> The amounts and concentrations do not change at equilibrium because, at the molecular level, reactants and products are reacting and forming at the same rate.

Changing the position of equilibrium

Changing concentration, pressure or temperature can change the position of the equilibrium of a reaction.

Changing concentration

If the concentration of a reactant is increased, the equilibrium will shift to the right to produce more products.

reactants ⇌ products

increasing concentration
of reactants shifts
equilibrium to the right

Changing pressure

If the pressure of an equilibrium mixture of gases is increased, the equilibrium will shift to the side of the reaction where there are the fewest moles.

Ammonia, NH_3, is manufactured by the Haber process:

$$N_2(g) +→ 3H_2(g) \rightleftharpoons 2NH_3(g)$$

There are four moles of gas on the left-hand side and only two moles on the right-hand side. Increasing the pressure shifts the equilibrium to the right to produce more NH_3.

> **Revision tip**
>
> The essential conditions for the Haber process are discussed on 118.

Changing the temperature

Increasing the temperature will shift the equilibrium in the direction of the endothermic reaction. Decreasing the temperature will shift the equilibrium in the exothermic direction.

In the manufacture of ammonia, the forward reaction is exothermic. Increasing temperature shifts the equilibrium to the left, decreasing the yield of ammonia.

> **Revision tip**
>
> If the forward reaction is exothermic, the reverse reaction is endothermic, e.g.
>
> $N_2(g) + 3H_2(g) \rightarrow 2NH_3(g)$
> exothermic (energy is given out)
>
> $2NH_3(g) \rightarrow N_2(g) + 3H_2(g)$
> endothermic (energy is taken in)

Quick test

1. Explain what the symbol ⇌ means in a chemical equation.
2. Describe what you would observe if water is added to anhydrous cobalt(II) chloride.

Supplement

3. Describe the characteristics of a reaction in equilibrium.
4. The equation for the manufacture of methanol, CH_3OH, is shown:

   $$CO(g) + 2H_2(g) \rightleftharpoons CH_3OH(g)$$

   The forward reaction is exothermic. Explain the effect of **(a)** increasing the pressure and **(b)** increasing the temperature on this reaction.

Redox reactions

Oxidation is the gain of oxygen, e.g. sulfur is oxidised in the reaction:

$S(s) + O_2(g) \rightarrow SO_2(g)$

Reduction is the loss of oxygen, e.g. copper oxide is reduced in the reaction:

$CuO(s) + H_2(g) \rightarrow Cu(s) + H_2O(l)$

Supplement

Transferring electrons

Oxidation **I**s **L**oss of electrons. **R**eduction **I**s **G**ain of electrons. (OIL RIG – see page 47.)

When zinc is added to copper(II) sulfate solution, the products are copper and zinc(II) sulfate:

$Zn(s) + CuSO_4(aq) \rightarrow Cu(s) + ZnSO_4(aq)$

This equation can be written as an ionic equation:

$Zn(s) + Cu^{2+}(aq) + SO_4^{2-}(aq) \rightarrow Cu(s) + Zn^{2+}(aq) + SO_4^{2-}(aq)$

$SO_4^{2-}(aq)$ appears on both sides of the ionic equation, so it doesn't take part in the reaction. It is called a **spectator ion** and is usually omitted:

$Zn(s) + Cu^{2+}(aq) \rightarrow Cu(s) + Zn^{2+}(aq)$

Zn has been oxidised because it has lost two electrons to form Zn^{2+}:
$Zn \rightarrow Zn^{2+} + 2e^-$

Cu^{2+} has been reduced because it has gained two electrons to form Cu:
$Cu^{2+} + 2e^- \rightarrow Cu$

This is a **redox reaction** because electrons are transferred and **red**uction and **oxi**dation take place in the same reaction:

- Zinc has reduced the copper(II) ions, so zinc is a **reducing agent**.
- Copper(II) ions have oxidised the zinc, so the copper(II) ion is an **oxidising agent**.

> **Revision tip**
>
> Deciding which substance is an oxidising agent and which is a reducing agent in a reaction can be confusing. From the equation, first determine which species has been oxidised and which has been reduced. Then it is fairly easy to work out which are the oxidising and reducing agents.

Oxidation states

Some metal ions have more than one charge.

The Roman numerals next to the name or symbol tell you the positive charge on the ion, e.g. copper(II) ions are Cu^{2+}. (See page 85 for other ions with more than one charge.)

The Roman numerals indicate the **oxidation state**, e.g. Fe^{2+} has an oxidation state of +2 and Fe^{3+} has an oxidation state of +3.

Supplement

Iron(II) chloride reacts with chlorine to form iron(III) chloride. The oxidation number has increased, which tells you that iron(II) ions have been oxidised to iron(III) ions.

Acidified potassium manganate(VII), $KMnO_4(aq) + H_2SO_4(aq)$, is a powerful oxidising agent:

- It is a purple solution due to the purple MnO_4^- ions.
- The (VII) tells you that manganese has an oxidation state of +7.
- When it oxidises a reactant, it changes to colourless manganese(II) ions, Mn^{2+}.
- You can tell the manganate(VII) ions have been reduced because there is a colour change from purple to colourless and the oxidation state decreases from +7 to +2.

Potassium iodide, KI, can be reduced to iodine, I_2:

- $2I^-(aq) \rightarrow I_2(aq) + 2e^-$
- Aqueous potassium iodide is a colourless solution, so iodide ions, I^-, are colourless.
- I^- ions have an oxidation state of −1.
- Iodine is red-brown in solution.
- I_2 is an element, so it has an oxidation state of zero.
- You can tell iodide ions have been oxidised because there is a colour change in the solution from colourless to red-brown and the oxidation state increases from −1 to 0.

Quick test

1. Explain which species is oxidised and which is reduced in the reaction:
   $Fe_2O_3(s) + 3CO(g) \rightarrow 2Fe(s) + 3CO_2(g)$

Supplement

2. Explain what is meant by *redox*.

3. Ethanol is oxidised by acidified potassium manganate(VII). What colour change would you observe in the reaction solution?

4. $Cl_2(aq) + 2Br^-(aq) \rightarrow 2Cl^-(aq) + Br_2(aq)$
   In this reaction identify the reactant that is **(a)** oxidised, **(b)** reduced, **(c)** the oxidising agent and **(d)** the reducing agent.

Exam-style practice questions

1 State whether each of the following changes is a **physical change** or a **chemical change**:

(a) dissolving copper(II) sulfate crystals in water to produce copper(II) sulfate solution   [1]

(b) adding dilute nitric acid to zinc to form zinc nitrate and hydrogen   [1]

(c) condensing ethanol vapour.   [1]

2 Calcium carbonate reacts with dilute hydrochloric acid to form carbon dioxide as one of the products:

$$CaCO_3(s) + 2HCl(aq) \rightarrow CaCl_2(aq) + H_2O(l) + CO_2(g)$$

A student investigates the rate of this reaction by measuring the volume of carbon dioxide given off.

(a) Draw the apparatus the student could use to measure the volume of carbon dioxide gas produced.   [2]

(b) The student records the following results:

Time / s	0	10	20	30	40	50	60	70	80	90	100	110
Volume of carbon dioxide / cm^3	0	9	18	26	32	38	42	not taken	48	49	50	50

Plot the points on graph paper and draw a smooth line of best fit.   [5]

(c) Estimate the volume of carbon dioxide at 70 s.   [1]

(d) Label your graph to show where the rate of reaction:

(i) is fastest   [1]

(ii) is slowing down   [1]

(iii) is zero.   [1]

(e) Explain why the rate of reaction slows down.   [1]

(f) Sketch another curve on the same axes to show the effect of using smaller pieces of calcium carbonate on the rate of this reaction.

Assume all other conditions are constant.   [2]

(g) Another student investigates the same reaction by measuring the mass lost.

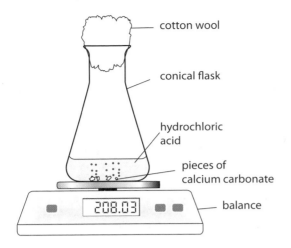

(i) Explain why mass is lost during this reaction. [1]

(ii) State what is observed in the reaction mixture during the reaction. [1]

(h) The student carries out two experiments using the apparatus in part (g).

The first experiment is carried out at 22 °C and the second is carried out at 30 °C.

All other factors are kept constant.

The student plots a graph of the results for the two temperatures.

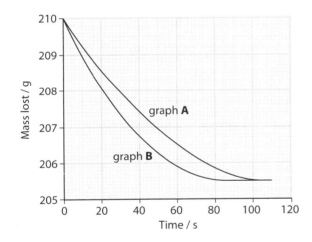

(i) State which graph, **A** or **B**, is carried out at 30 °C.

Explain your reasoning. [2]

(ii) Determine the total mass lost in both experiments. [1]

(iii) Calcium carbonate is in excess in this reaction.

Suggest an observation that confirms this. [1]

(iv) Explain why the total mass lost is the same for both experiments. [1]

Supplement

(v) Explain, in terms of collisions between particles, why increasing the temperature of a reaction increases the rate. [2]

3 Light can affect the rate of some chemical reactions.

(a) State the products of photosynthesis. [1]

(b) Name the plant pigment that is required for photosynthesis to take place. [1]

(c) In photography, silver salts are used to coat photographic film.

    (i) Give the ionic half-equation to show the reaction that occurs when light reaches the silver salt coating. [1]

    (ii) Explain why this equation shows reduction has taken place. [1]

4 Hydrated copper(II) sulfate crystals, $CuSO_4.5H_2O$, are blue.

(a) What would you observe when the crystals are heated for some time? [1]

(b) Describe how you could remake hydrated copper(II) sulfate crystals after they have been heated. [1]

(c) Write an equation showing this reversible reaction. [2]

Supplement

5 Iodine monochloride will take part in a reversible reaction with chlorine to form iodine trichloride:

$$ICl(l) \quad + \quad Cl_2(g) \quad \rightleftharpoons \quad ICl_3(s)$$
brown liquid   pale green gas   yellow solid

Chlorine is passed into a glass U-tube containing iodine monochloride and the U-tube is sealed.

After an hour, an equilibrium is established at room temperature and all three compounds are present.

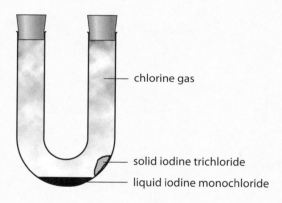

    — chlorine gas

    — solid iodine trichloride
    — liquid iodine monochloride

(a) Explain why this reaction reaches *equilibrium*. [1]

(b) Explain what is meant by the term equilibrium. [2]

(c) What observation could you make to confirm this reaction is at equilibrium? [1]

(d) Explain what would happen to the equilibrium if the pressure inside the U-tube was increased. [2]

(e) The temperature inside the U-tube is raised to 40 °C.

The brown liquid increases in volume and the quantity of yellow solid is much less.

Explain how these observations show that the forward reaction is exothermic. [2]

6 An important equilibrium reaction in the manufacture of nitric acid is the formation of nitrogen monoxide:

$$4NH_3(g) + 5O_2(g) \rightleftharpoons 4NO(g) + 6H_2O(g)$$

The forward reaction is exothermic.

Predict the conditions of pressure and temperature that would give the maximum yield of nitrogen monoxide.

Explain the reasons for the conditions you choose. [4]

7 Lead can be extracted from its ore by the following reaction:

$$PbO(s) + C(s) \rightarrow Pb(s) + CO(g)$$

Identify the substance that has been oxidised and the substance that has been reduced in this reaction.

Explain the reasons for your answers. [2]

Supplement

8 Astatine, At, is a very rare element. It gives the following reaction with iodine:

$$I_2(aq) + 2At^-(aq) \rightarrow 2I^-(aq) + At_2(aq)$$

Identify and explain which substance is oxidised and which substance is reduced in this reaction. [4]

9 Acidified potassium manganate(VII) acts as an oxidising reagent in many reactions.

(a) Explain what is meant by the term oxidising agent. [1]

(b) State the colour change that would be observed when acidified potassium manganate(VII) acts as an oxidising agent. [2]

(c) In a redox reaction, manganate(VII) ions form manganese(II) ions.

Explain why manganese has been reduced in this reaction. [1]

Acids

Aqueous solutions can be acidic, alkaline or neutral. Indicators can show which by changing colour:

- Litmus is red in acidic solutions and blue in alkaline solutions.
- Methyl orange is red in acidic solutions and yellow in alkaline solutions.
- Universal Indicator gives a range of colours that show how strong or weak **acids** and **alkalis** are. The scale of numbers in the diagram below is the **pH scale**.

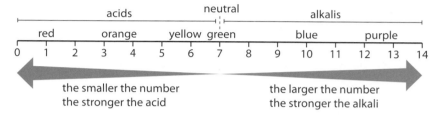

Acidic solutions have a pH less than 7. The stronger the acidic solution, the smaller the number.

Alkaline solutions have numbers greater than 7. The closer to pH 14, the stronger the alkaline solution.

A neutral solution is exactly pH 7, e.g. sodium chloride solution.

Characteristic reactions of acids

Here are some common acids:

- hydrochloric acid, HCl
- nitric acid, HNO_3
- phosphoric acid, H_3PO_4
- sulfuric acid, H_2SO_4
- ethanoic acid, CH_3COOH.

The first four are **strong acids** and have a pH of 1 or 2.

Ethanoic acid is a **weak acid** with a pH of 3 or 4.

Reaction with metals

Acids react with most metals to give a **salt** and hydrogen:

metal + acid → salt + hydrogen

For example:

zinc + sulfuric acid → zinc sulfate + hydrogen
$$Zn(s) + H_2SO_4(aq) \rightarrow ZnSO_4(aq) + H_2(g)$$

In this reaction, bubbles are observed. This is hydrogen being given off.

The test for hydrogen is a lighted splint – it will give a squeaky pop.

Revision tip

When testing a solution using Universal Indicator paper or litmus paper, a glass rod is dipped into the solution and a spot is put on the paper. This way, the solution is not contaminated by the dyes in the paper. To determine the pH using Universal Indicator, the colour of the paper is compared to a colour chart

Revision tip

In the practical exam, you may be asked what you observed in an experiment. If you see bubbles (effervescence), this is the observation. Saying that you see hydrogen gas is incorrect – this is a deduction from your observation.

Reaction with bases

Metal oxides and hydroxides are **bases** (see page 79). Acids react with these compounds to form a salt and water:

$$\text{base} \quad + \quad \text{acid} \quad \rightarrow \quad \text{salt} \quad + \text{water}$$

For example:

- copper(II) oxide + hydrochloric acid → copper(II) chloride + water

$$CuO(s) \quad + \quad 2HCl(aq) \quad \rightarrow \quad CuCl_2(aq) \quad + H_2O(l)$$

- magnesium hydroxide + nitric acid → magnesium nitrate + water

$$Mg(OH)_2(s) \quad + 2HNO_3(aq) \rightarrow \quad Mg(NO_3)_2(aq) \quad + H_2O(l)$$

These are called neutralisation reactions (see page 80).

Reaction with carbonates

Acids react with carbonates to from a salt, water and carbon dioxide:

$$\text{carbonate} \quad + \quad \text{acid} \quad \rightarrow \quad \text{salt} \quad + \text{water} + \text{carbon dioxide}$$

For example:

magnesium carbonate + sulfuric acid → magnesium sulfate + water + carbon dioxide

$$MgCO_3(s) \quad + \quad H_2SO_4(aq) \quad \rightarrow \quad MgSO_4(aq) \quad + H_2O(l) + \quad CO_2(g)$$

When this reaction takes place, bubbles (fizzing or effervescence) will be seen because carbon dioxide is produced.

The test for carbon dioxide is limewater – it turns milky.

Supplement

Acids only show acidic properties in water, i.e. aqueous solutions.

They form hydrogen ions, $H^+(aq)$, e.g.

$$HNO_3(aq) \rightarrow H^+(aq) + NO_3^-(aq)$$

Strong acids are fully ionised in water (aqueous solution). Nitric acid is a strong acid.

Weak acids do not fully ionise in aqueous solutions – they only partly ionise. Ethanoic acid is a weak acid because only some ethanoic acid molecules form ions, e.g.

$$CH_3COOH(aq) \rightleftharpoons CH_3COO^-(aq) + H^+(aq)$$

Acids are proton (H^+) donors.

Revision tip

Hydrogen has an atomic number of 1, so it has one proton and one electron. A H^+ ion is a proton because the electron has been removed leaving the hydrogen nucleus (1 proton). See page 13 for more information.

Quick test

1. Citric acid forms a weak acidic solution. State what colour changes you would observe with:

   (a) blue litmus paper

   (b) red litmus paper

   (c) universal Indictor paper

   (d) methyl orange.

2. Write the formula for each of these strong acids:

   (a) nitric acid

   (b) sulfuric acid

   (c) phosphoric acid

   (d) hydrochloric acid.

3. Write the word equation for the reaction of magnesium with sulfuric acid.

4. What is the test for the gas produced when copper(II) carbonate reacts with nitric acid?

Supplement

5. Write the equations for the reactions in Questions 3 and 4.

6. Write the equation for the formation of $H^+(aq)$ ions in dilute sulfuric acid.

Revision tip

If you are asked to write an equation in an exam, this means a balanced equation.

Characteristic reactions of bases

Bases are substances that react with acids to produce salts and water. This is called **neutralisation**.

Metal oxides and metal hydroxides are bases and so is ammonia.

If a base dissolves in water it is an **alkali**.

Definition
Alkalis are soluble bases.

For example, aqueous sodium hydroxide, NaOH(aq), and aqueous ammonia, $NH_3(aq)$, are alkalis.

Some common bases
Insoluble bases:

* copper(II) oxide, CuO
* zinc oxide, ZnO
* magnesium hydroxide, $Mg(OH)_2$.

Soluble bases (alkalis):

* sodium hydroxide, NaOH
* potassium hydroxide, KOH
* calcium hydroxide, $Ca(OH)_2$.

Reaction with acids

Bases react with acids to form a salt and water:

base + acid → salt + water.

Two examples of this type of reaction were given on page 77. Here are some more examples:

* zinc oxide + sulfuric acid → zinc sulfate + water
  $$ZnO(s) + H_2SO_4(aq) → ZnSO_4(aq) + H_2O(l)$$

* sodium hydroxide + nitric acid → sodium nitrate + water
  $$NaOH(aq) + HNO_3(aq) → NaNO_3(aq) + H_2O(l)$$

* ammonia + hydrochloric acid → ammonium chloride
  $$NH_3(aq) + HCl(aq) → NH_4Cl(aq)$$

This ammonia reaction is more complicated and does not produce water, but ammonium chloride is still called a salt.

These are neutralisation reactions because the acid and alkali cancel (neutralise) each other.

Controlling soil acidity
Most plants grow best when the soil pH is close to 7.

Farmers neutralise acidic soils with lime (calcium oxide, CaO) and slaked lime (calcium hydroxide, $Ca(OH)_2$). See page 87 for more information about these compounds and how they are made.

Reaction with ammonium salts

All alkalis, except ammonia, react with ammonium salts, e.g.

sodium hydroxide + ammonium chloride → sodium chloride + water + ammonia

$$NaOH(aq) + NH_4Cl(aq) \rightarrow NaCl(aq) + H_2O(l) + NH_3(g)$$

Ammonia has a pungent odour (strong smell).

The test for ammonia is damp red litmus paper – it turns blue.

Supplement

In water, alkalis produce hydroxide ions, $OH^-(aq)$, e.g.

$$KOH(aq) \rightarrow K^+(aq) + OH^-(aq)$$

Strong bases are fully ionised in water (aqueous solution). Potassium hydroxide is a strong base.

Weak bases do not fully ionise in aqueous solutions – they only partly ionise. Ammonia is a weak base because only some ammonia molecules form ions:

$$NH_3(aq) + H_2O(l) \rightleftharpoons NH_4^+(aq) + OH^-(aq)$$

Neutralisation and proton transfer

When an acid reacts with an alkali, H^+ ions from the acid react with OH^- ions from the alkali:

$$H^+(aq) + OH^-(aq) \rightarrow H_2O(l)$$

This reaction occurs in all acid-alkali reactions, e.g.

$$NaOH(aq) + HNO_3(aq) \rightarrow NaNO_3(aq) + H_2O(l)$$

This can be written as an ionic equation:

$$\cancel{Na^+(aq)} + OH^-(aq) + H^+(aq) + \cancel{NO_3^-(aq)} \rightarrow \cancel{Na^+(aq)} + \cancel{NO_3^-(aq)} + H_2O(l)$$

> **Revision tip**
>
> **Spectator ions** do not take part in the reaction and occur on both sides of equations. They are usually omitted from ionic equations, so we write:.
> $OH^-(aq) + H^+(aq) \rightarrow H_2O(l)$.

Because this reaction involves the loss and gain of H^+ ions, it is known as proton transfer.

The acid donates a proton to the OH^- ion of the alkali.

Bases are known as proton acceptors because they accept protons from acids.

Quick test

1. Explain what is meant by the term alkali.
2. Give the name and formulae of **three** bases.
3. Name the salt formed when lead(II) oxide reacts with nitric acid.
4. **(a)** Explain why it is important to control the acidity of soils.
   (b) Name and give the formula of **two** compounds a farmer can use to neutralise an acidic soil.
5. Describe the test for ammonia gas.

Supplement

6. State the ion present in all alkaline solutions.
7. Explain why ammonia forms a weak alkaline solution in water.
8. Write the ionic equation for an acid reacting with an alkali.

Types of oxide

When elements react with oxygen they form oxides.

Metal elements react to give metal oxides, e.g.

- magnesium + oxygen → magnesium oxide
  $2Mg(s) + O_2(g) → 2MgO(s)$

- sodium + oxygen → sodium oxide
  $4Na + O_2(g) → 2Na_2O(s)$

All metal oxides are ionic solids.

If the metal oxide dissolves in water, the solution produced is alkaline.

MgO is slightly soluble in water. It gives a pH of 8 and turns red litmus blue.

Sodium oxide dissolves completely in water to give sodium hydroxide, $NaOH(aq)$, with a pH of 13:

$Na_2O(s) + H_2O(l) → 2NaOH(aq)$

Non-metal elements react to give non-metal oxides, e.g.

sulfur + oxygen → sulfur dioxide (sulfur is a non-metal)
$S(s) + O_2(g) → SO_2(g)$

Many non-metals oxides are gases and most dissolve to give acidic solutions.

For example, sulfur dioxide, from burning fossil fuels that contain sulfur compounds, is a major contributor to acid rain (see page 114).

Revision tip

Remember, metal oxides are basic oxides because they react with acids to make salts and water.

Revision tip

Remember, non-metal oxides react with bases to form a salt + water.

Supplement

Amphoteric oxides react with both acids and bases to make salts + water. Aluminium oxide, Al_2O_3, is an amphoteric oxide.

Neutral oxides do not react with acids or bases. Water, H_2O, and carbon monoxide, CO, are neutral oxides.

Quick test

1. Which of these compounds are acidic oxides?
   A nitrogen dioxide, NO_2
   B lithium oxide, Li_2O
   C calcium oxide, CaO
   D chlorine(I) oxide, Cl_2O.

2. Write the word equation for the reaction of lead(II) oxide with dilute nitric acid.

Supplement

3. Write the balanced equation for the reaction in Question 2.
4. Nitrogen monoxide, NO, is a neutral oxide. Explain what the term *neutral* means.

Salts are metal compounds made from acids.

They are named using the name of the metal and part of the name of the acid:

- Hydro**chlor**ic acid produces **chlor**ides.
  The H of HCl is replaced by the metal, e.g. sodium chloride, NaCl.
- **Nit**ric acid produces **nitr**ates.
  The H of HNO_3 is replaced by the metal, e.g. potassium nitrate, KNO_3.
- **Sulf**uric acid produces **sulf**ates.
  The Hs in H_2SO_4 are replaced by the metal, e.g. zinc sulfate, $ZnSO_4$.
- **Phosph**oric acid produces **phosph**ates.
  The Hs in H_3PO_4 are replaced by the metal, e.g. aluminium phosphate, $AlPO_3$.

Ammonium salts are made by reacting aqueous ammonia with acids, e.g. ammonium sulfate, $(NH_4)_2SO_4$, is made from ammonia and sulfuric acid.

Making soluble salts from a solid base, carbonate or metal

1. Add the solid to the acid until no more reacts. Heating may be required.

2. Filter off the excess solid into an evaporating dish.

3. Evaporate the water by heating gently until the solution is ready to crystallise, i.e. when the solution is saturated with the salt. This is the crystallisation point.

4. Leave the solution to cool and form crystals.

5. Filter the crystals and leave them to dry.

> **Revision tip**
>
> To see if a substance is ready to crystallise, a glass rod is dipped into the solution and removed. If crystals form on the glass rod, the solution is at the right concentration to form crystals.

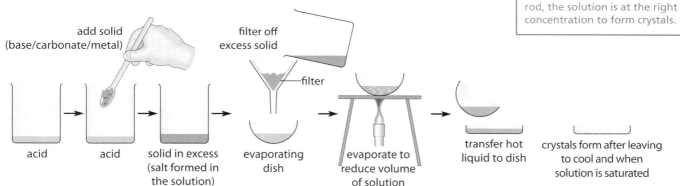

add solid (base/carbonate/metal)   filter off excess solid   filter

acid   acid   solid in excess (salt formed in the solution)   evaporating dish   evaporate to reduce volume of solution   transfer hot liquid to dish   crystals form after leaving to cool and when solution is saturated

Making a soluble salt from an alkali

Alkalis are soluble bases. In the previous method, the excess solid could be seen, which meant the reaction was complete. In this case, both reactants and products are colourless solutions, so titration is used to produce the salt solution.

1. Use a pipette to accurately measure the volume of alkali – usually 25.0 cm³.

2. Put the alkali in a conical flask and add a few drops of indictor solution.

3. Fill a burette with acid and note the initial volume. Burettes measure volumes of solutions accurately.

4. Allow the acid to run into the conical flask until the indicator just changes colour. This is the neutralisation point. Note the final volume to find out how much acid has been used.

5. Repeat Steps **1–3** without adding indicator and use the burette to deliver the exact volume of acid used in Step **4**.

6. Evaporate the solution to the crystallisation point and allow to crystallise (as in Step **4** of the previous experiment). Then filter and leave the crystals to dry.

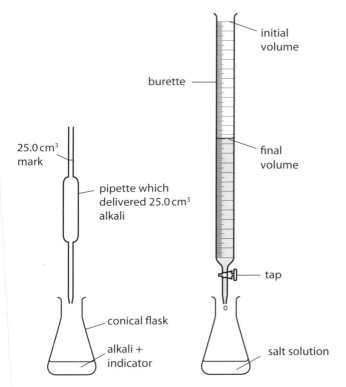

Revision tip

Here is an easy way to remember the reactions that make salts:
A (acid) + A (alkali)
A (acid) + B (base)
A (acid) + C (carbonate)
A (acid) + M (metal)

Supplement

Preparing an insoluble salt

To prepare an insoluble salt, you do not need to use an acid:

- Choose two solutions.
- One should contain the metal ion (cation) of the salt you are preparing.
- The other solution should contain the negative ion (anion) of the salt you are preparing.
- Mix the two solutions and a precipitate forms. This is the insoluble salt.

Silver iodide, AgI, is an insoluble salt that can be prepared using the following method:

1. Mix two solutions, one containing silver ions, $Ag^+(aq)$, and one containing $I^-(aq)$ ions.
2. A precipitate of silver iodide forms and is filtered.
3. The precipitate in the filter paper is washed with water and allowed to dry.

The ionic equation for this reaction is: $Ag^+(aq) + I^-(aq) \rightarrow AgI(s)$

Revision tip

A precipitate is an insoluble solid in a liquid.

Revision tip

All nitrates are soluble salts in water, so a suitable silver salt solution would be silver nitrate, $AgNO_3$.
All Group I salts are soluble in water, so a suitable iodide solution would be potassium iodide.

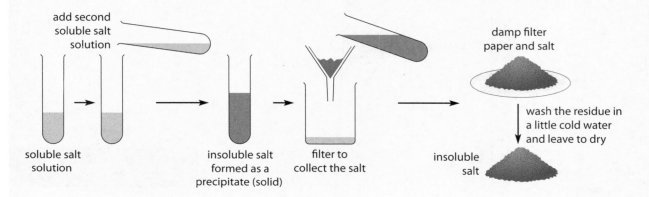

add second soluble salt solution

soluble salt solution

insoluble salt formed as a precipitate (solid)

filter to collect the salt

damp filter paper and salt

insoluble salt

wash the residue in a little cold water and leave to dry

Quick test

1. What is the name of the salt formed when zinc and hydrochloric acid are reacted together?
2. Explain how you could prepare calcium chloride using an excess of insoluble calcium carbonate.
3. Potassium hydroxide is an alkali. Describe the method you would use to prepare potassium sulfate from aqueous potassium hydroxide.
4. Copy and complete this word equation:

   potassium hydroxide + ... → potassium sulfate + ...

Supplement

5. All nitrates are soluble. All potassium salts are soluble. Use this information to choose **two** soluble salts to prepare insoluble lead(II) bromide.

Identifying ions and gases

Identifying metal ions (cations) with flame tests

1. Dip a flame test wire into water.
2. Dip the damp flame test wire into the solid compound.
3. Put it in the edge of a blue Bunsen flame and note the flame colour.

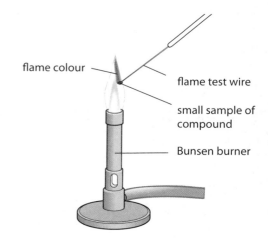

flame colour — flame test wire

small sample of compound

Bunsen burner

Flame test colours of cations (positive ions)

Cation	Formula	Flame colour
lithium	Li^+	red
sodium	Na^+	yellow
potassium	K^+	lilac
copper(II)	Cu^{2+}	blue-green

Identifying aqueous cations using aqueous sodium hydroxide and aqueous ammonia

Some cations in solution form insoluble hydroxides. These can be precipitated with sodium hydroxide solution, NaOH(aq).

Some of the hydroxide precipitates are coloured and some are white.

Adding aqueous ammonia, NH_3(aq), to cations in solution often produces the same colour precipitate as using sodium hydroxide in some instances but sometimes the results are different.

Tests for cations (positive ions)

Cation	Formula	Effect of adding NaOH(aq)	Effect of adding NH_3(aq)
aluminium	Al^{3+}	white ppt. of $Al(OH)_3$ dissolves in excess to give a colourless solution	white ppt. of $Al(OH)_3$ does not dissolve in excess
calcium	Ca^{2+}	white ppt. of $Ca(OH)_2$ does not dissolve in excess	no ppt. (or only a very slight white ppt.)
chromium(III)	Cr^{3+}	green ppt. of $Cr(OH)_3$ dissolves in excess	grey-green ppt. of $Cr(OH)_3$ does not dissolve in excess
copper(II)	Cu^{2+}	light blue ppt. does not dissolve in excess	light blue ppt. dissolves in excess to give dark blue solution
iron(II)	Fe^{2+}	green ppt. of $Fe(OH)_2$ does not dissolve in excess	green ppt. of $Fe(OH)_2$ does not dissolve in excess
iron(III)	Fe^{3+}	red-brown ppt. of $Fe(OH)_3$ does not dissolve in excess	red-brown ppt. of $Fe(OH)_3$ does not dissolve in excess
zinc	Zn^{2+}	white ppt. of $Zn(OH)_2$ dissolves in excess to give a colourless solution	white ppt. of $Zn(OH)_2$ dissolves in excess to give colourless solution

The ammonium ion, NH_4^+, is also a cation. If a solution containing these ions is warmed with aqueous sodium hydroxide, ammonia gas is produced, which has a pungent odour (smell) and turns damp red litmus paper blue.

Identifying negative ions (anions)

Carbonate ions, CO_3^{2-}, in solid or solution give carbon dioxide, CO_2, when dilute acid is added. Effervescence (fizzing) is observed and CO_2 turns limewater milky (see page 77).

Sulfite ions, SO_3^{2-}, in solid or in solution give sulfur dioxide gas, SO_2, when warmed with dilute acid. SO_2 gas has a pungent, choking odour and turns acidified aqueous potassium manganate(VII), MnO_4^-, from purple to colourless.

The tests for other anions in solution are shown in the table below:

Revision tip

SO_2 reduces MnO_4^- to Mn^{2+}. There are two ways you can tell this is a reduction reaction: there is a colour change from purple to colourless and a decrease in oxidation state from +7 to +2 (see page 135).

Anion	Formula	Test	Result
chloride	Cl^-	• add a few drops of dilute nitric acid, HNO_3, to acidify • then add a few drops of aqueous silver nitrate, $AgNO_3$	white ppt. of AgCl
bromide	Br^-		cream ppt. of AgBr
iodide	I^-		yellow ppt. of AgI
nitrate	NO_3^-	• add aqueous sodium hydroxide, NaOH(aq) • then add aluminium foil and warm gently	ammonia gas is produced, which turns red litmus blue
sulfate	SO_4^{2-}	• add a few drops of dilute nitric acid, HNO_3, to acidify • then add aqueous barium nitrate, $Ba(NO_3)_2$(aq)	white ppt. of $BaSO_4$

Revision tip

The tests for cations and anions shown here look slightly different to those at the back of the syllabus and Paper 5. This is because the extra detail may be required in Papers 1–4.

Identifying gases

Gas	Formula	Test
ammonia	NH_3	turns damp red litmus blue
carbon dioxide	CO_2	turns limewater milky
chlorine	Cl_2	bleaches damp litmus paper (turns the litmus paper white)
hydrogen	H_2	gives a squeaky pop with a lighted splint
oxygen	O_2	relights a glowing splint
sulfur dioxide	SO_2	acidified aqueous potassium manganate(VII), turns from purple to colourless

Quick test

1. What flame colour is observed when a few crystals of lithium nitrate are heated using a Bunsen burner?
2. Compound Q gives a red-brown precipitate with aqueous ammonia. State which metal ion is present.
3. Outline the procedure you could use to test for sulfate anions in a solid salt.
4. Describe the test you perform to show carbon dioxide gas is present.

Supplement

5. Write an ionic equation for the reaction of aqueous iron(III) ions with aqueous sodium hydroxide. Include state symbols.

Limestone is calcium carbonate, $CaCO_3$. Marble is also calcium carbonate, $CaCO_3$.

Carbonates contain CO_3^{2-}.

Carbonates react with acids to give a salt, water and carbon dioxide.

Metal carbonates undergo **thermal decomposition** (are broken down by heat) to give the metal oxide and carbon dioxide.

For limestone, this is a very important reaction. It is carried out in a lime kiln at high temperature. Lime, which is calcium oxide, is produced:

$$\text{calcium carbonate} \xrightarrow{\text{heat}} \text{calcium oxide} + \text{carbon dioxide}$$

$$\underset{\text{limestone}}{CaCO_3(s)} \xrightarrow{\text{heat}} \underset{\text{lime}}{CaO(s)} + CO_2(g)$$

A rotary lime kiln is one type of kiln in which limestone is heated to very high temperatures to produce lime.

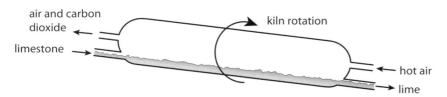

If water is added to lime a very exothermic reaction occurs to give slaked lime, which is calcium hydroxide, $Ca(OH)_2$:

$$\text{calcium oxide} + \text{water} \rightarrow \text{calcium hydroxide}$$
$$CaO(s) + H_2O(l) \rightarrow Ca(OH)_2(s)$$

Uses of limestone, lime and slaked lime

Limestone, $CaCO_3$	Lime, CaO, and slaked lime, $Ca(OH)_2$
• making cement: powdered limestone is heated with powdered clay • limestone is used in the blast furnace during the extraction of iron: limestone decomposes to calcium oxide, CaO, in the heat. CaO then reacts with acidic impurities like silicon dioxide (sand) and removes them as molten slag, calcium silicate	• neutralising soil acidity • neutralising acidic waste, e.g. removing sulfur dioxide, responsible for acid rain, from industrial flue gases

> **Revision tip**
>
> Buildings made of limestone or marble are damaged by acid rain because it reacts with carbonates (see page 114).

> **Revision tip**
>
> Remember, in **exothermic** reactions heat energy **exits** (see page 56).

> **Revision tip**
>
> Lime and slaked lime have similar uses because they both react with acids.

Quick test

1. State the chemical name and formula of limestone.
2. Write the chemical equation for the production of lime.
3. State **two** uses of slaked lime.
4. Write the word equation for the formation of slaked lime from lime.
5. Explain why it is important to remove sulfur dioxide from flue gases.

Exam-style practice questions

1 Dilute phosphoric acid, H_3PO_4, shows the typical properties of a strong acid.

   (a) Describe what you would observe when a drop of dilute phosphoric acid is placed on blue litmus paper. [1]

   (b) A drop of Universal Indicator solution is added to a small volume of dilute phosphoric acid in a test tube.

   State the colour you would observe and explain what this indicates about its pH number. [2]

   (c) Complete the word equation:

   magnesium + phosphoric acid → .... + ... [2]

   (d) Zinc carbonate reacts with dilute phosphoric acid.

   (i) State what is observed during the reaction. [1]

   (ii) Name the salt solution that is formed. [1]

Supplement

   (e) Acids only react as typical acids in aqueous solution.

   (i) Complete the equation:

   $H_3PO_4(aq) \rightarrow$ ....(aq) + ...(aq) [2]

   (ii) How does the equation in part (i) show why dilute phosphoric acid shows acidic properties? [1]

   (iii) Explain why ethanoic acid is a weak acid. [1]

2 One of the typical properties of bases is that they react with acids.

   (a) Complete the general equation:

   base + acid → .... + ... [1]

   (b) State the name of **two** bases that would form magnesium chloride. [2]

   (c) Another typical property of a base is that it will react with ammonium salts to give a pungent smelling gas.

   (i) Give the name and formula of the gas produced. [2]

   (ii) Describe a test to identify this gas. [2]

3 The table gives the soil pH ranges in which certain species of trees grow best.

Tree species	pH range
American beech	5.0–6.5
birch	5.0–6.0
holly	4.5–5.5
honey locust	6.0–8.0
maple	6.0–7.5

(a) Identify the tree species that grows best over the largest range of pH values. [1]

(b) Identify **two** tree species that grow best in neutral soils. [1]

(c) Describe a method for testing the pH of a soil. [3]

(d) Explain how are acidic soils are neutralised. [1]

Supplement

4 Ammonia solution reacts with hydrochloric acid:

$$NH_3(aq) + HCl(aq) \rightarrow NH_4^+(aq) + Cl^-(aq)$$

Use ideas about proton transfer to explain how ammonia is acting as a base and hydrochloric acid is acting as an acid. [3]

5 Four oxides are listed below:

aluminium oxide   carbon monoxide   lead(II) oxide   phosphorus(V) oxide

From these four oxides identify which:

(a) dissolves in water to form a solution that has a pH of less than 7 [1]

(b) does not react with acids or bases [1]

(c) reacts with both acids and bases to form salts. [1]

6 Copper(II) sulfate is a soluble blue salt that can be made from solid copper(II) oxide using dilute sulfuric acid.

(a) Write the word equation for this reaction. [1]

(b) Copper(II) oxide is added to the sulfuric acid until it is in excess.

State the observation that can be made when copper(II) oxide is in excess. [1]

(c) Explain how excess copper(II) oxide is removed from the solution of copper(II) sulfate at the end of the reaction. [2]

(d) Outline the procedure to produce pure dry copper(II) sulfate crystals from the copper(II) sulfate solution. [4]

(e) Another compound that can be used to form copper(II) sulfate is solid copper(II) carbonate.

(i) State one observation that is made during this reaction that is different to the reaction between copper(II) oxide and dilute sulfuric acid. [1]

(ii) Complete the chemical equation. There is no need to add state symbols.

$CuCO_3 + H_2SO_4 \rightarrow$ .... + ... + ... [2]

7 Aqueous sodium hydroxide reacts with dilute ethanoic acid to form the salt sodium ethanoate.

A student prepares this salt. She uses a pipette to deliver 25.0 cm³ of sodium hydroxide solution into a conical flask.

(a) What should she add to the sodium hydroxide solution in the flask at the start of the experiment before adding the acid? [1]

(b) What piece of equipment should she use to measure the volume of ethanoic acid that exactly neutralises the sodium hydroxide solution? [1]

(c) What observation is made when the sodium hydroxide solution is exactly neutralised by the ethanoic acid? [1]

Supplement

8 Silver bromide is an insoluble salt.

(a) Outline the procedure for preparing pure silver bromide from the soluble salt, silver nitrate. [5]

(b) Write the ionic equation for this reaction and include state symbols. [2]

9 Limestone is heated in a lime kiln to produce lime:

$$CaCO_3(s) \rightleftharpoons CaO(s) + CO_2(g)$$

(a) What does the symbol $\rightleftharpoons$ mean in this equation? [1]

(b) Describe the type of reaction that occurs when lime is formed. [1]

(c) Carbon dioxide can react with lime.

Explain why this is called an acid-base reaction. [3]

(d) Slaked lime is formed when lime is reacted with water.

(i) Give the chemical formula of slaked lime. [1]

(ii) Write the chemical equation for the formation of slaked lime from lime. [1]

(e) State **two** uses of limestone other than for making lime. [2]

The Periodic Table

The Periodic Table is the chemist's way of classifying elements (see page 16):

- Elements are placed in order of **proton number**.
- They are arranged in **periods** (horizontal rows) and **groups** (columns).
- There are eight groups and all the elements in a group have similar chemical properties.
- The middle block of elements is called the **transition elements**.
- An element's position in the Periodic Table can be used to predict its properties.

Groups	I	II											III	IV	V	VI	VII	VIII
Periods																		
1						1 H hydrogen												2 He helium
2	3 Li lithium	4 Be beryllium											5 B boron	6 C carbon	7 N nitrogen	8 O oxygen	9 F fluorine	10 Ne neon
3	11 Na sodium	12 Mg magnesium				transition elements							13 Al aluminium	14 Si silicon	15 P phosphorus	16 S sulfur	17 Cl chlorine	18 Ar argon
4	19 K potassium	20 Ca calcium	21 Sc scandium	22 Ti titanium	23 V vanadium	24 Cr chromium	25 Mn manganese	26 Fe iron	27 Co cobalt	28 Ni nickel	29 Cu copper	30 Zn zinc	31 Ga gallium	32 Ge germanium	33 As arsenic	34 Se selenium	35 Br bromine	36 Kr krypton
5	37 Rb rubidium	38 Sr strontium	39 Y yttrium	40 Zr zirconium	41 Nb niobium	42 Mo molybdenum	43 Tc technetium	44 Ru ruthenium	45 Rh rhodium	46 Pd palladium	47 Ag silver	48 Cd cadmium	49 In indium	50 Sn tin	51 Sb antimony	52 Te tellurium	53 I iodine	54 Xe xenon
6	55 Cs caesium	56 Ba barium	57 La lanthanum	72 Hf hafnium	73 Ta tantalum	74 W tungsten	75 Re rhenium	76 Os osmium	77 Ir iridium	78 Pt platinum	79 Au gold	80 Hg mercury	81 Tl thallium	82 Pb lead	83 Bi bismuth	84 Po polonium	85 At astatine	86 Rn radon

Key

proton number (atomic number)
atomic symbol
name

metal | non metal

Metals and non-metals

Elements can be classified as metals or non-metals.

Most elements are metals and are to the left of the zig-zag line shown on the Periodic Table above.

Metallic character changes to non-metallic character across a period.

Physical properties of metals and non-metals

Metals	Non-metals
shiny appearance	dull appearance
solids (except mercury which is liquid)	about half are solids and half are gases (except bromine, which is liquid)
high melting points (except, e.g. Group 1)	melting points are often low
high densities (except, e.g. Group 1)	low densities
good conductors of electricity	poor conductors of electricity (except carbon graphite) – they are insulators
good conductors of heat	poor conductors of heat
malleable (can be bent and hammered into shape)	brittle when solid (break when hammered)

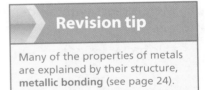

> **Revision tip**
>
> Many of the properties of metals are explained by their structure, **metallic bonding** (see page 24).

Alloys

Metals are malleable because the layers of atoms can slide over one another.

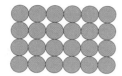 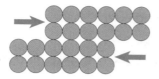

> **Definition**
>
> An **alloy** is a mixture of a metal and at least one other element.

In alloys, the atoms are different sizes, which disrupts the layered structure of the pure metal. The layers cannot slide over each other making them harder.

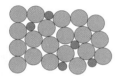

Aluminium, copper and iron are alloyed with other elements to change their properties.

Alloy	Elements mixed together	Change in property and use
brass	varying mixtures of copper and zinc	• stronger than copper, but brasses are still very good electrical conductors • can be used in electrical fittings
duralumin	96% aluminium, 4% copper and other metals	• stronger than aluminium, but still with low density • used in aircraft manufacture
stainless steel	iron with at least 11% chromium and other elements, e.g. nickel	• corrosion resistant and stronger than iron • used in cutlery

Two chemical properties of metals

1. Metals react with oxygen to form metal oxides, which are ionic solids, e.g.

    calcium + oxygen → calcium oxide
    $$2Ca(s) + O_2(g) \rightarrow 2CaO$$

2. Metals react with acids to form salts and hydrogen (see page 82), e.g.

    zinc + nitric acid → zinc nitrate + hydrogen
    $$Zn + 2HNO_3 \rightarrow Zn(NO_3)_2 + H_2(g)$$

Remember, metal oxides are basic and non-metal oxides are acidic (see page 81).

Supplement

Electronic structure and the Periodic Table

It is important to recall how electrons are arranged in atoms and how this relates to the Periodic Table (see page 16).

Some characteristics of the groups in the Periodic Table

Group number	I	II	III	IV	V	VI	VII	VIII
Electrons in outer shell	1	2	3	4	5	6	7	8 (2 for He)
Ion charge	1+	2+	3+	typically no ions	3–	2–	1–	no ions
Metallic or non-metallic	metallic			non-metallic at top of group	non-metallic			
Reactivity	reactivity increases ←				reactivity increases →			unreactive

Revision tip

Remember, metal atoms lose electrons to form positive ions. Non-metals gain electrons to form negative ions.

Quick test

1. Which element is found in Group IV of Period 2?
2. Describe **three** physical properties of metals.
3. Explain what is meant by the term *alloy*.
4. Describe **two** chemical properties of metals.

Supplement

5. What is the charge on a Group VII ion?

Group I

Group I elements – the **alkali metals** – become more reactive going down the group.

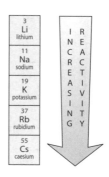

Physical properties

Lithium, sodium and potassium are the three metals you are most likely to come across from this group. They are metals with unusual physical properties:

- They are soft compared to most metals and can be cut with a knife.
- They are shiny when cut but this quickly dulls as they react with gases in the air.
- They have low densities and float on water (most metals sink!). Densities increase going down the group.
- Their melting points are low compared to most metals and decrease going down the group. Look at the table below and compare these to the melting point of iron, 1540 °C.

Element	Melting point / °C
Li	180
Na	98
K	63

Chemical properties

The alkali metals are chemically very reactive. They react with water and air, which is why they are stored under oil.

They also react with other elements, e.g.

- with chlorine: sodium + chlorine → sodium chloride

  $2Na(s) + Cl_2(g) \rightarrow 2NaCl(s)$

- with oxygen: sodium + oxygen → sodium oxide

  $4Na(s) + O_2(g) \rightarrow 2Na_2O(s)$

They become more reactive going down the group.

Reaction with water

Alkali metals float and react with water.

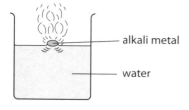

alkali metal

water

They float, fizz (effervesce) and move around. The fizzing is due to hydrogen gas being formed.

Reactivity increases going down the group:

- Lithium fizzes much less vigorously than sodium or potassium and it does not melt.
- Sodium produces enough heat to melt, so it forms a molten ball of metal as it moves around the surface of the water.

- The reaction of water with potassium is so exothermic that the potassium melts into a molten ball and the hydrogen catches fire and burns with a lilac flame.

The solution formed is alkaline due to formation of alkaline metal hydroxides, e.g.

potassium + water → potassium hydroxide + hydrogen

$$2K(s) + 2H_2O(l) \rightarrow 2KOH(aq) + H_2(g)$$

Predicting the properties of other Group I elements

Like every group in the Periodic Table, the alkali metals have similar properties, which usually show a trend.

You can use this knowledge to make predictions about other Group I elements. For example, rubidium will be a soft metal that reacts very violently with water.

Revision tip

Metal oxides and metal hydroxides are bases.
If bases are soluble in water, then they are called alkalis.
It is the hydroxide ion, $OH^-(aq)$, that causes the aqueous solutions to be alkaline.

Supplement

Chemical reactions only involve electrons in the outer shell.

Group I metals have similar chemical reactions because they all have one electron in their outer shell. They are very reactive because they can easily lose this one electron to leave a full outer shell.

Reactivity increases going down Group I because the atoms get bigger. This means the outer, negative electron is further from the attraction of the positive nucleus, so it is more easily lost.

Quick test

1. State **three** physical properties of Group 1 elements.
2. Use the table on page 94 to predict the melting point of rubidium, which is below potassium in Group I.
3. Give the word and balanced equation for the reaction of sodium with water.
4. Describe the trend in reactivity of the alkali metals going down Group I.

Supplement

5. Explain why Group I elements all show similar chemical properties.

Transition elements

The **transition elements** are not a group. They are a block of metals between Groups II and III:

- They have similar properties.
- They are all metals, which is why they are often called transition metals.
- They behave like typical metals, unlike the metals in Group I.

Property	Transition metal	Group I metal
Melting point	high	low
Density	high	low
Colour of compounds	coloured	white
Reaction with water	slow or no reaction	vigorous
Reaction with acid	usually slow or no reaction	violent

Transition elements form coloured compounds, e.g.

- iron(II) hydroxide, $Fe(OH)_2$, is green
- iron(III) hydroxide, $Fe(OH)_3$, is brown (see 'Tests for cations' on page 85).

Transition elements and their compounds often act as **catalysts**, e.g.

- iron is a catalyst in the **Haber process** for the manufacture of ammonia (see page 118):
  $$N_2(g) + 3H_2(g) \rightleftharpoons 2NH_3(g)$$
- vanadium(V) oxide, V_2O_5, catalyses the Contact process for the manufacture of sulfuric acid (see page 106):
  $$2SO_2(g) + O_2(g) \rightleftharpoons 2SO_3(g)$$

Revision tip

Remember, catalysts increase the rate of reactions but are chemically unchanged at the end.

Supplement

Transition elements have variable oxidation states.

For example, iron has two oxidation states, +2 and +3, because it forms Fe^{2+} and Fe^{3+}. This is seen in iron(II) hydroxide, $Fe(OH)_2$, and iron(III) hydroxide, $Fe(OH)_3$.

Quick test

1. Copy and complete the following sentences:

   (a) Transition elements have .... densities and .... melting points.

   (b) Transition elements form .... compounds.

   (c) Transition elements are .... reactive than Group 1 metals.

   (d) Transition elements and their compounds often act as ....

2. Where in the Periodic Table would you find the transition elements?

3. (a) Define the term *catalyst*.

   (b) What important industrial process uses iron as a catalyst?

Supplement

4. Iron forms two compounds with chlorine. Iron(II) chloride is a green salt and iron(III) chloride is a brown salt. Give **two** reasons why this information shows that iron is a transition element.

Group VII and Group VIII

Group VII elements – the halogens

Group VII elements (the **halogens**) become less reactive going down the group.

Chlorine, bromine and iodine are non-metals and the ones you are most likely to come across from this group.

They are diatomic molecules.

Their properties and trends going down the group are shown in the table below:

Halogen molecule	Colour and state at room temperature	Trend in colour	Trend in density
Cl_2	pale green gas	darker down group	density increases down group
Br_2	red-brown liquid		
I_2	grey-black solid		

The halogens are chemically very reactive and reactivity decreases going down the group.

Displacement reactions

A more reactive element will displace a less reactive element from its compounds. These are called **displacement reactions**.

Chlorine is more reactive than bromine:

- When chlorine is added to a solution of sodium bromide, it displaces (takes the place of) bromine.
- The solution turns orange due to the displaced bromine and sodium chloride is formed.
- chlorine + sodium bromide → sodium chloride + bromine
  $$Cl_2(aq) + 2NaBr(aq) \rightarrow 2NaCl(aq) + Br_2(aq)$$

Chlorine is also more reactive than iodine:

- When chlorine is added to sodium iodide solution, iodine is displaced and the solution looks dark orange/brown.
- chlorine + sodium iodide → sodium chloride + iodine
  $$Cl_2(aq) + 2NaI(aq) \rightarrow 2NaCl(aq) + I_2(aq)$$

Supplement

These equations can be written ionically. As Na^+ is on both sides of the equation and does not take part in the reaction, it is called a **spectator ion** and does not need to be included.

For example, chlorine reacts with aqueous sodium bromide:

$$Cl_2(aq) + 2Br^-(aq) \rightarrow 2Cl^-(aq) + Br_2(aq)$$

This is a redox reaction because:

- Cl_2 gains electrons: $Cl_2 + 2e^- \rightarrow 2Cl^-$. It is reduced.
- Br^- loses electrons: $2Br^- \rightarrow Br_2 + 2e^-$. It is oxidised.

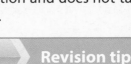

Revision tip

Remember, **OIL RIG**: Oxidation is loss of electrons. Reduction is gain of electrons.

Group VII elements have similar chemical reactions because they all have 7 electrons in their outer shell.

They are very reactive because they can easily gain one electron to achieve a noble gas configuration of full shells.

Reactivity decreases going down Group VII because the atoms get larger, so the positive nucleus cannot easily attract an extra negative electron.

Group VIII elements – the noble gases

The noble gases are in Group VIII, which can also be called Group 0.

These non-metal elements are all unreactive:

- This is because their atoms have full outer shells, which are stable. They do not lose, gain or share electrons easily (see page 93).
- This is also why they exist as single atoms, i.e. they are monatomic.

Because noble gases are unreactive, they can provide an inert (unreactive) atmosphere, e.g. helium is used to fill balloons and argon is used in lamps.

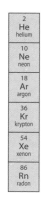

| 2 |
| He |
| helium |
| 10 |
| Ne |
| neon |
| 18 |
| Ar |
| argon |
| 36 |
| Kr |
| krypton |
| 54 |
| Xe |
| xenon |
| 86 |
| Rn |
| radon |

Quick test

1. Describe the trend in reactivity of the halogens going **down** Group VII.
2. Copy and complete the following sentences:

    (a) The elements in Group VII are called the ....

    (b) Group VII elements all have .... atoms in their molecules so their molecules are called ....

    (c) The Group VII elements .... and .... are gases. Bromine is a .... and iodine is a ....

    (d) The colour of the Group VII elements becomes .... down the group.
3. Explain what is meant by a *displacement reaction*.
4. Give the word and balanced equation for the displacement reaction between bromine and potassium iodide solution, KI(aq).
5. State the name of the Group VIII or Group 0 elements.
6. Explain why the Group VIII or Group 0 elements are unreactive.

Supplement

7. (a) Write the ionic equation for the reaction between chlorine and iodide ions.

    (b) Explain which reactant is oxidised and which is reduced in the reaction in part (a).

Reactivity series

Metals can be placed in a league table with the most reactive metals at the top. It is called a **reactivity series**.

The more reactive a metal is:

- the more easily it forms compounds
- the harder it is to break its compounds down.

Notice that in the reactivity series, on the right of this page, we have included hydrogen and carbon. The reasons for doing this will be explained later in this section.

Potassium	K
Sodium	Na
Calcium	Ca
Magnesium	Mg
Aluminium	Al
(Carbon	C)
Zinc	Zn
Iron	Fe
(Hydrogen	H)
Copper	Cu

increasing reactivity

Reactions with water or steam and with dilute hydrochloric acid

Element	Symbol	Reaction with water or steam	Reaction with dilute HCl
potassium	K	fizz in cold water, giving off hydrogen gas and forming alkaline hydroxide solution	violent – explosive
sodium	Na		
calcium	Ca		
magnesium	Mg	react with steam to produce hydrogen gas and metal oxide	fizz giving off hydrogen gas: metal + acid → salt + hydrogen
zinc	Zn		For example:
iron	Fe		$Zn + 2HCl \rightarrow ZnCl_2 + H_2$
(hydrogen)	(H)		
copper	Cu	no reaction with steam	no reaction with HCl(aq)

Hydrogen is included in the reactivity series because metals above it are more reactive than hydrogen and can displace it from water or acid, e.g.

magnesium + steam → magnesium oxide + hydrogen
$Mg(s) + H_2O(g) \rightarrow MgO(s) + H_2(g)$

Copper does not react with water, steam or dilute hydrochloric acid because it is below hydrogen in the reactivity series.

 Revision tip

This reaction is like the displacement reactions of the halogens (see page 97). The more reactive element, magnesium, is displacing the less reactive element, hydrogen, from its compound, water.
The test for hydrogen is a lighted splint – the gas gives a squeaky pop.

Reduction of metal oxides with carbon

Carbon is included in the reactivity series to show how it can be used to extract some metals from their metal oxide ores.

Carbon will displace metals below it from their metal oxides, e.g.

copper(II) oxide + carbon → copper + carbon dioxide
$2CuO(s) + C \rightarrow 2Cu(s) + CO_2(g)$

 Revision tip

Remember that copper(II) oxide is reduced because it loses oxygen and carbon is oxidised because it gains oxygen (see page 70).

Supplement

Displacement reactions

A metal's position in the reactivity series depends on how easily it forms positive ions.

The metals at the top of the reactivity series form ions much more easily than those at the bottom.

A metal higher up the reactivity series will displace a metal lower down from its compound.

Metals displacing other metals from their oxides

Aluminium displaces iron from iron(III) oxide because aluminium forms ions more easily than iron:

aluminium + iron(III) oxide → aluminium oxide + iron

$2Al$ + Fe_2O_3 → Al_2O_3 + $2Fe$

This reaction is so exothermic, it melts the iron!

$Al \rightarrow Al^{3+} + 3e^-$

Oxidation of Al (loss of electrons) and oxidation state increases from 0 to +3.

$Fe^{3+} + 3e^- \rightarrow Fe$

Reduction of Fe^{3+} (gain of electrons) and oxidation state decreases from +3 to 0.

Metals displacing other aqueous metal ions

A more reactive metal will also displace a less reactive metal from a solution of its salts.

For example, magnesium ribbon is put into aqueous copper(II) sulfate, which is a blue solution.

Very quickly:

* the silvery magnesium ribbon becomes coated with a brown substance
* the blue colour of the solution fades to colourless.

Magnesium is more reactive than copper, so it forms aqueous Mg^{2+} ions more easily than the copper does.

The magnesium displaces the aqueous Cu^{2+} and forms magnesium sulfate solution.

— aqueous copper(II) sulfate

— magnesium ribbon

The blue colour of copper(II) fades as brown copper and colourless magnesium ions form:

magnesium +   copper(II) sulfate   →   magnesium sulfate + copper

$Mg(s)$ + $Cu^{2+}(aq) +$ ~~$SO_4^{2-}(aq)$~~ → $Mg^{2+}(aq) +$ ~~$SO_4^{2-}(aq)$~~ + $Cu(s)$

As sulfate ions are spectator ions, the equation is often written without SO_4^{2-}:

$Mg(s) + Cu^{2+}(aq) \rightarrow Mg^{2+}(aq) + Cu(s)$

The reverse reaction does not happen because Cu is below Mg in the reactivity series.

The action of heat on carbonates, hydroxides, and nitrates

The more reactive a metal is, the more stable its compounds are to heat.

The effect of heat on carbonates and hydroxides

The more reactive a metal is, the more stable its compounds are to thermal decomposition, e.g. sodium carbonate will not decompose even at high temperatures but copper(II) carbonate decomposes on gentle heating.

> **Revision tip**
>
> If a compound is broken down into simpler substances by heat, the process is called **thermal decomposition**.

Revision tip

Calcium carbonate (limestone) needs very high temperatures to decompose to calcium oxide (lime). This is why lime kilns need to operate at very high temperatures (see page 87).

Reactivity series	Symbol	Effect of heat on the metal carbonate	Effect of heat on the metal hydroxide
potassium	K	do not decompose – stable to heat	do not decompose – stable to heat
sodium	Na		
calcium	Ca	$CaCO_3 \rightarrow CaO + CO_2$	$Ca(OH)_2 \rightarrow CaO + H_2O$
magnesium	Mg	$MgCO_3 \rightarrow MgO + CO_2$	$Mg(OH)_2 \rightarrow MgO + H_2O$
zinc	Zn	$ZnCO_3 \rightarrow ZnO + CO_2$	$Zn(OH)_2 \rightarrow ZnO + H_2O$
iron	Fe	$FeCO_3 \rightarrow FeO + CO_2$	$2Fe(OH)_3 \rightarrow Fe_2O_3 + 3H_2O$
copper	Cu	$CuCO_3 \rightarrow CuO + CO_2$	$Cu(OH)_2 \rightarrow CuO + H_2O$

The effect of heat on nitrates

Reactivity series	Symbol	Effect of heat on the metal nitrate	Notes
potassium	K	$2KNO_3 \rightarrow 2KNO_2 + O_2$	nitrate → nitrite + oxygen
sodium	Na	$2NaNO_3 \rightarrow 2NaNO_2 + O_2$	
calcium	Ca	$2Ca(NO_3)_2 \rightarrow 2CaO + 4NO_2 + O_2$	nitrate → oxide + nitrogen dioxide + oxygen
magnesium	Mg	$2Mg(NO_3)_2 \rightarrow 2MgO + 4NO_2 + O_2$	
zinc	Zn	$2Zn(NO_3)_2 \rightarrow 2ZnO + 4NO_2 + O_2$	
iron	Fe	$2Fe(NO_3)_2 \rightarrow 2FeO + 4NO_2 + O_2$	nitrogen dioxide is a brown gas
copper	Cu	$2Cu(NO_3)_2 \rightarrow 2CuO + 4NO_2 + O_2$	

With very strong heating, potassium nitrate and sodium nitrate will decompose to the nitrite only.

As with the thermal decomposition of the carbonates and hydroxides, less energy is required as the metals become less reactive.

Why does aluminium appear so unreactive?

Aluminium is more reactive than zinc. However, its surface is protected by a thin layer of aluminium oxide, which means it does not react with dilute acids and does not displace less reactive metal ions in solution (see page 49).

Quick test

1. Copy and complete this word equation: calcium + water → .... + ...
2. Explain why copper does not react with dilute hydrochloric acid.
3. Copy and complete this equation: Mg + ... HCl → .... + ...
4. Write the word equation for the reduction of zinc oxide by carbon.

Supplement

5. Explain why a strip of zinc put into lead(II) nitrate solution becomes coated with a dark grey substance. Write an ionic equation for the reaction that takes place.
6. State the name of the solid compound formed when sodium nitrate is heated.

Extraction of metals

An **ore** is rock containing a high proportion of metal or metal compound.

Metals are extracted from their ores.

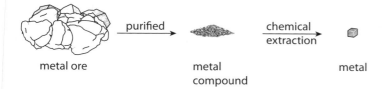

metal ore → purified → metal compound → chemical extraction → metal

The method used to extract a metal from its compound depends on its position in the reactivity series.

The most reactive metals, which are above carbon in the reactivity series, are extracted by electrolysis, e.g. aluminium from bauxite (see page 48).

Element	Symbol	Extraction method
potassium	K	electrolysis
sodium	Na	
calcium	Ca	
magnesium	Mg	
aluminium	Al	
carbon	C	
zinc	Zn	using carbon or carbon monoxide
iron	Fe	
copper	Cu	using carbon or other methods

Extracting iron

The iron ore, called hematite, contains iron(III) oxide, Fe_2O_3. It is mixed with coke (carbon) and limestone and fed into a **blast furnace**.

Zone 1:
- Blasts of hot air start the reaction.
- Coke (carbon) burns to form carbon dioxide: $C(s) + O_2(g) \rightarrow CO_2(g)$
  This is an exothermic reaction, so it increases the temperature in the furnace.

Zone 2:
- Unreacted coke then forms carbon monoxide, CO:
  carbon + carbon dioxide → carbon monoxide
  $$C(s) + CO_2(g) \rightarrow 2CO(g)$$

Zone 3:
- Fe_2O_3 is reduced by carbon monoxide to produce molten iron:
  iron(III) oxide + carbon monoxide → iron + carbon dioxide
  $$Fe_2O_3(s) + 3CO(g) \rightarrow 2Fe(l) + 3CO_2(g)$$

The molten iron trickles down and is collected at the bottom of the furnace.

Limestone is used to remove sand and other impurities as molten slag.

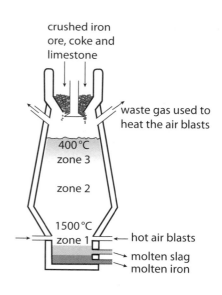

crushed iron ore, coke and limestone

waste gas used to heat the air blasts

400°C zone 3

zone 2

1500°C zone 1

hot air blasts

molten slag
molten iron

In the heat of the furnace, limestone is decomposed to form lime (calcium oxide):

calcium carbonate → calcium oxide + carbon dioxide

$$CaCO_3(s) \rightarrow CaO(s) + CO_2(g)$$

limestone   lime

Revision tip

Remember, metal carbonates, such as calcium carbonate, undergo thermal decomposition to produce metal oxides and carbon dioxide.

Calcium oxide is basic and reacts with silicon dioxide (sand), which is acidic, to form molten calcium silicate (slag):

Calcium oxide + silicon dioxide → calcium silicate

$$CaO(s) + SiO_2(s) \rightarrow CaSiO_3(l)$$

            sand   slag

The slag floats on top of the iron at the bottom of the furnace and is removed.

Molten iron is released at the bottom of the blast furnace. It is called cast iron.

It has about 4% carbon in it, which makes it very brittle. The carbon comes from the coke and there are also other impurities.

Making steel

Most of the iron from the blast furnace is converted to steel, which has less carbon in it than cast iron. Other impurities are also removed. This is done in the **basic oxygen process**.

Removal of carbon:

* Oxygen is blown through the molten iron from the blast furnace and the carbon in it reacts to form carbon dioxide: $C(s) + O_2(g) \rightarrow CO_2(g)$
* CO_2 is a gas, so it escapes.

Removal of other impurities:

* silicon: silicon + oxygen → silicon dioxide

  $$Si(s) + O_2(g) \rightarrow SiO_2(s)$$
* phosphorus: phosphorus + oxygen → phosphorus(V) oxide

  $$4P(s) + 5O_2(g) \rightarrow P_4O_{10}(s)$$
* The oxides formed are non-metal oxides, so they are acidic.
* Calcium oxide is added together with the molten iron into the furnace.
* It is a basic oxide – hence the word 'basic' in the basic oxygen process.
* Calcium oxide reacts with these acidic oxides:

  calcium oxide + silicon dioxide → calcium silicate

  calcium oxide + phosphorus(V) oxide → calcium phosphate
* These salts form molten slag, which floats on the molten steel.

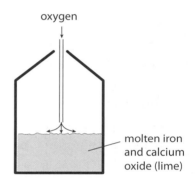

oxygen

molten iron and calcium oxide (lime)

Different steels

Steel is the name given to various **alloys** of iron. Two of these are mild steel and stainless steel:

* Mild steel is used to make car bodies and machinery.
* Stainless steel is resistant to corrosion and is used to make cutlery and in chemical plants.

Revision tip

An alloy is a mixture of a metal and at least one other element. The properties of the metal are changed by the other elements added. You can read more about this on page 92.

The properties of pure iron are changed by adding controlled amounts of carbon and other elements. Steel alloys contain 0.1–1.5% carbon.

The more carbon there is in the steel, the stronger and harder it is.

Mild steel contains approximately 0.3% of carbon. It is malleable and easily shaped.

High carbon steel contains approximately 2% carbon. It is harder and less malleable than mild steel. It is used for hammers, chisels and railway tracks.

Other transition elements are added to improve strength and corrosion resistance, e.g. stainless steel contains at least 11% chromium and other elements, such as nickel.

Rusting of iron and its prevention

When iron corrodes, it is called rusting. For iron and steel to rust, both air and water must be present.

To prevent rusting, water or oxygen, or both, must be stopped from reaching the iron's surface. This can be done by coating the iron with paint or a thin layer of tin or plastic.

Supplement

Another way of preventing rust is **sacrificial protection**, where a metal higher up the reactivity series reacts with air and water instead of the iron.

For example, zinc or magnesium blocks are fixed to the hulls of ships so that they corrode leaving the iron hull rust free.

If zinc is used to coat iron, it is called **galvanising**. The zinc provides a protective coating. Even if this is scratched, so that iron is exposed, the zinc will corrode first.

Recycling iron and steel

Just as with aluminium (see page 49), it makes sense to recycle iron and steel:

- Less ore needs to be mined, so there is less local environmental damage.
- Less energy is used – the blast furnace uses huge quantities of energy and this energy is mostly supplied by burning non-renewable fossil fuels.
- It is less polluting because less fossil fuels are used, so not as much carbon dioxide (a greenhouse gas) goes into the atmosphere.

Supplement
Extracting zinc

Zinc sulfide, ZnS, is found in an ore called zinc blende. This is heated in air to form zinc oxide and sulfur dioxide:

$$2ZnS + 3O_2 \rightarrow 2ZnO + 2SO_2$$

Zinc oxide is reduced to zinc by heating with carbon in the form of coke. Carbon monoxide is formed:

$$ZnO + C \rightarrow Zn + CO$$

This is done in a furnace that is very similar to the blast furnace used for the extraction of iron.

The furnace gets very hot. Zinc has a lower melting point than iron, so it boils and vaporises at the top of the furnace where it is condensed and collected.

> **Revision tip**
>
> The sulfur dioxide produced in this process can be used to manufacture sulfuric acid (see page 106).

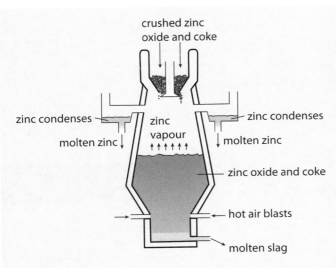

Zinc is used in the alloy brass where it is mixed with copper (see page 92) and to galvanise iron.

Quick test

1. What is the meaning of the term ore?
2. Name the process that is used to extract reactive metals, such as aluminium.
3. List the **four** raw materials used to extract iron in the blast furnace.
4. Write the word equation for the reduction of iron(III) oxide with carbon monoxide.
5. Explain why lime is added together with molten iron in the basic oxygen process.
6. Explain how oxygen removes carbon in the basic oxygen process. Include a word and balanced equation in your answer.
7. Steel cans are electroplated with a thin coating of tin. Explain how this prevents rusting.

Supplement

8. Write the balanced equation for the reduction reaction in Question 4.
9. Outline the **two** main stages in the extraction of zinc from zinc blende. Write balanced equations for the reactions that occur.
10. (a) What is meant by the term *galvanising*?

    (b) Explain how the galvanising prevents rusting.

Sulfur

Sulfur is in Group VI of the Periodic Table. It is an important non-metal.

The main sources of sulfur are:

- metal sulfide ores, e.g. zinc blende, ZnS
- sulfur-containing fossil fuels
- uncombined in the ground.

Most of the sulfur produced is used to manufacture sulfuric acid, H_2SO_4.

Sulfur dioxide, SO_2, is used:

- to bleach wood pulp for making paper
- as a food preservative, because it kills bacteria.

Revision tip

Sulfur dioxide is largely responsible for acid rain (see page 114).

Supplement

Manufacturing sulfuric acid by the Contact process

There are three stages to manufacturing sulfuric acid by the Contact process:

> **Stage 1 – Burning sulfur in air to make sulfur dioxide**
>
> $S(s) + O_2(g) \rightarrow SO_2(g)$

> **Stage 2 – Making sulfur trioxide**
>
> $2SO_2(g) + O_2(g) \rightleftharpoons 2SO_3(g)$
>
> Conditions:
> V_2O_5 catalyst; 450 °C; 1–2 atmospheres pressure

> **Stage 3 – Making sulfuric acid**
>
> The sulfur trioxide is first dissolved in concentrated H_2SO_4, to make oleum, $H_2S_2O_7$:
>
> $SO_3(g) + H_2SO_4(l) \rightarrow H_2S_2O_7(l)$.
>
> Water is added to oleum to make sulfuric acid:
>
> $H_2S_2O_7(l) + H_2O(l) \rightarrow 2H_2SO_4(l)$

Revision tip

You must learn the reaction conditions in Stage 2 and all of the equations.

Stage 2 is an equilibrium reaction:

- The reaction is exothermic, so you would expect a low temperature to be used to shift the equilibrium to the right. However, this makes the reaction too slow, so 450 °C is used.
- There are fewer moles of gas on the right, so you would expect a high pressure to shift the equilibrium to the right. However, a low pressure is used because the yield is 98 per cent at 1–2 atmospheres.
- Using vanadium(V) oxide does not change the position of the equilibrium, but it increases the rate of the forward and reverse reactions so the equilibrium is achieved faster.

Revision tip

In Stage 2 we are considering the effect of changing conditions on the position of equilibrium. See page 69 for an explanation of the principles involved.

Stage 3:

- Water could be added directly to sulfur trioxide to make sulfuric acid:

    $SO_3(g) + H_2O(l) \rightarrow H_2SO_4(aq)$

    However, the reaction is too dangerous because it is very exothermic.
- Instead, sulfur trioxide is added to concentrated sulfuric acid to make oleum, $H_2S_2O_7$.
- The oleum is then reacted with water to make sulfuric acid. This is a safer, less violent reaction.

Properties and uses of dilute sulfuric acid

Dilute sulfuric acid has the characteristic properties of acids (see pages 76 and 77).

Uses of dilute sulfuric acid:

- Manufacturing the fertiliser ammonium sulfate, $(NH_4)_2SO_4$:
    - Add aqueous ammonia to dilute sulfuric acid.
      $NH_3(aq) + H_2SO_4(aq) \rightarrow (NH_4)_2SO_4(aq)$
    - Evaporate the water to obtain crystals of ammonium sulfate.
- Cleaning metal surfaces.

Properties and uses of concentrated sulfuric acid

Concentrated sulfuric acid contains no water, so does not act as an acid.

Properties of concentrated sulfuric acid:

- It is very corrosive and can cause severe burns.
- It is a strong oxidising agent.
- It is a dehydrating agent (removes water from compounds).
  When concentrated sulfuric acid is added to sucrose (sugar), $C_{12}H_{22}O_{11}$, it removes all the H and O atoms as water and dehydrates it to black carbon:

  $C_{12}H_{22}O_{11}(s) \xrightarrow{\text{conc. } H_2SO_4} 12C(s) + 11H_2O(g)$

Uses of concentrate sulfuric acid:

- Making explosives.
- Making dyes.

Quick test

1. State **two** main sources of sulfur.
2. What is the major use of sulfur?
3. State **two** uses of sulfur dioxide.

Supplement

4. Give the equation and the reaction conditions for the formation of sulfur trioxide from sulfur dioxide in the Contact process.
5. State the name and formula of the substance formed when sulfur trioxide is dissolved in concentrated sulfuric acid.
6. Water is added to the substance formed in Question **5**. Write the equation for this reaction.
7. Explain why sugar turns black when concentrated sulfuric acid is added.
8. Give **two** uses of concentrated sulfuric acid.

Exam-style practice questions

1 Some of the elements and their positions in the Periodic Table are shown.

Li																	
	Mg											Al				Cl	Ar
								Ni								Br	

In answering these questions, each element can be used once, more than once, or not all.

Which element:

(a) has a very high density? [1]

(b) is a red-brown liquid at room temperature? [1]

(c) floats on water? [1]

(d) is a diatomic gas at room temperature? [1]

(e) has a full outer shell of electrons? [1]

(f) displaces another element in the same group from its compounds? Both elements are shown in the Periodic Table above. [1]

2 Potassium has a violent reaction with water.

(a) Complete the word equation for the reaction:

potassium + water → .... + ... [2]

(b) A very small piece of potassium is placed in a bowl of water.

Give **three** observations that can be made during this experiment. [3]

(c) At the end of the reaction described in part (b), some Universal Indicator solution is added to the water in the bowl.

(i) What is the colour of Universal Indicator in the water? [1]

(ii) What does this show about the pH of the water at the end of the reaction? [1]

(d) Name an element in the same group as potassium that has a less violent reaction with water. [1]

Supplement

(e) Explain why potassium always forms an ion with a charge of +1. [2]

(f) Give the chemical equation for the reaction of lithium with water. Include state symbols. [2]

3 Astatine is the rarest naturally occurring element on Earth. It is produced by the radioactive decay of other elements and lasts for just a few hours before decaying.

Its properties can be predicted because it is a member of Group VII.

The properties of some of the Group VII elements are shown in the table.

Element	Melting point / °C	Boiling point / °C	Colour	State at room temperature
chlorine	−101	−34	pale green	gas
bromine	−7	+59	red-brown	liquid
iodine	+114	+184	grey-black	solid
astatine				

(a) Use information in the table to explain why bromine is a liquid. [1]

(b) Predict the colour and state of astatine. [1]

(c) Suggest a melting point and boiling point for astatine. [2]

(d) Predict how the reactivity of astatine will compare to iodine. Explain your answer. [2]

(e) Astatine has a symbol At. Predict the formula of a molecule of astatine. [1]

Supplement

(f) Predict how many electrons will be in astatine's outer shell? [1]

(g) Predict the charge on the astatide ion. [1]

4   One of the typical properties of metals is that they are malleable.

(a) State what is meant by the term *malleable*. [1]

(b) Explain how the structure of a metal allows it to be malleable. [2]

(c) When iron is first extracted from its ore in the blast furnace it is very strong but not very malleable. This is because it is alloyed with approximately 4% carbon.

Define the term *alloy*. [1]

(d) Explain why iron from the blast furnace is not malleable. [2]

5   Iron reacts with steam in this apparatus.

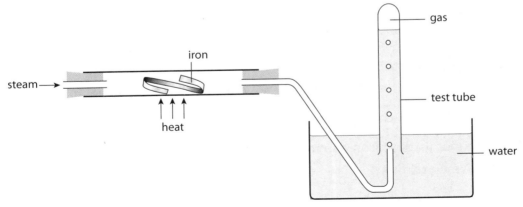

(a) Name the gas that is collecting in the test tube. [1]

(b) Suggest the identity of the solid compound formed in the heated tube. [1]

(c) Write a word equation for the reaction. [1]

(d) Calcium reacts violently with steam but reacts steadily with cold water.

The gas is collected and gives a squeaky pop with a lighted splint.

Complete this chemical equation:

Ca(s) + ... → ....(aq) + ...(g) [2]

(e) Copper shows no reaction with steam.

Place **iron**, **calcium** and **copper** in order of their reactivity with steam, starting with the most reactive first. [1]

(f) What is observed if copper is placed in a solution of dilute sulfuric acid? [1]

Supplement

6 The results of two experiments are represented by these word equations:

tin + lead(II) oxide → tin(II) oxide + lead

nickel + tin(II) oxide → nickel(II) oxide + tin

(a) Place the metals, **tin**, **lead** and **nickel**, in order of their reactivity, putting the most reactive metal first. [1]

(b) Write the chemical equation for the reaction of tin with lead(II) oxide. [2]

(c) Two test tubes were set up. Each contained a zinc strip.

Into **test tube 1** was poured aqueous iron(II) nitrate, a green solution.

Into **test tube 2** was poured aqueous magnesium nitrate, a colourless solution.

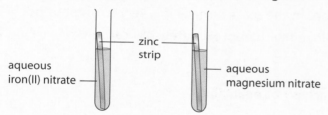

zinc strip

aqueous iron(II) nitrate

aqueous magnesium nitrate

After one hour these observations were made:

- The zinc in **test tube 1** was coated by a dark grey layer and the green solution had turned colourless.
- There was no change in **test tube 2**.

(i) Explain the observations in **test tube 1**. Your answer should include an ionic equation. [3]

(ii) Explain why there was no change observed in **test tube 2**. [2]

(iii) Place the three metals, zinc, iron and magnesium, in order of reactivity, putting the most reactive metal first. [1]

7 Iron is extracted from its ore in a blast furnace. A diagram of the blast furnace is shown.

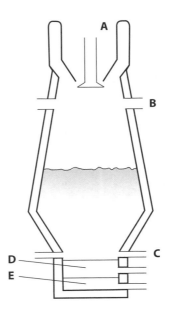

(a) State the name of the iron ore. [1]

(b) (i) Name **two** other raw materials that are mixed with the iron ore before it enters the blast furnace. [2]

(ii) At which place, **A**, **B** or **C**, does this mixture of raw materials enter the blast furnace? [1]

(iii) At which place, **A**, **B** or **C**, do blasts of hot air enter the furnace? [1]

(c) (i) What label should be written at **D**? [1]

(ii) What label should be written at **E**? [1]

(d) In the furnace, carbon burns in blasts of air to form carbon dioxide.

Write the chemical equation for this reaction. You need not use state symbols. [1]

(e) The carbon dioxide reacts with more carbon to form carbon monoxide.

Write the chemical equation for this reaction. You need not use state symbols. [1]

(f) Iron is formed when iron(III) oxide reacts with carbon monoxide.

(i) Balance the equation for this reaction.

$Fe_2O_3(s)$ + ...$CO(g)$ → ....$Fe(l)$ + ...$CO_2(g)$ [1]

(ii) Explain why iron(III) oxide is reduced in this reaction. [1]

(g) Iron from the blast furnace contains impurities. These are removed in the basic oxygen furnace and steel is made.

(i) Oxygen is blown into the molten iron. Explain how this removes some of the carbon impurity. [2]

(ii) Phosphorus and silicon are two other impurities. Explain how these are removed. Include one chemical equation for a reaction with oxygen and one word equation for a reaction with calcium oxide. [4]

Water

Chemical tests for water

There are two tests that you can carry out to see if a liquid contains water:

Anhydrous copper(II) sulfate, CuSO$_4$
Add the liquid to anhydrous copper(II) sulfate (CuSO$_4$). This white powder turns blue if water is present:

$$CuSO_4(s) + 5H_2O(l) \rightleftharpoons CuSO_4.5H_2O(s)$$
white solid   blue solid

Anhydrous cobalt(II) chloride, CoCl$_2$
Add the liquid to anhydrous cobalt(II) chloride (CoCl$_2$). This blue compound turns pink if water is present:

$$CoCl_2(s) + 6H_2O(l) \rightleftharpoons CoCl_2.6H_2O(s)$$
blue solid   pink solid

Blue cobalt chloride paper is often used. Filter paper is soaked in a solution of cobalt chloride, which is pink, and the filter paper is heated until it turns blue.

Dropping a liquid containing water onto the blue cobalt chloride paper turns it back to pink.

These reversible reactions were covered on page 68.

> ### Revision tip
> These tests confirm that water is present in the liquid. To find out if the liquid is pure water, you need to check that it melts at exactly 0°C or boils at exactly 100°C.

Making water safe to drink

The human body contains about sixty percent water by mass and we will not survive very long without drinking water.

Making sure water is safe to drink can be a matter of life and death, so water supplies are treated to make them safe.

The two main processes are filtration and chlorination.

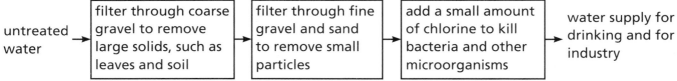

untreated water → filter through coarse gravel to remove large solids, such as leaves and soil → filter through fine gravel and sand to remove small particles → add a small amount of chlorine to kill bacteria and other microorganisms → water supply for drinking and for industry

> ### Revision tip
> Remember, chlorine, Cl$_2$, is an element found in Group VII of the Periodic Table.

Uses of water

Apart from using water in the home for drinking, cooking and washing, water is essential to many industrial processes:

- It is an excellent **solvent** and many reactions take place when reactants are dissolved in aqueous solution, e.g.
  ammonium nitrate salt, NH_4NO_3, is an important fertiliser made by reacting ammonia solution with nitric acid solution and then evaporating the water away.
- It is an important cheap **raw material**, e.g.
  it is a source of hydrogen for the manufacture of ammonia by the Haber process (see page 118).
- It is a **coolant**, e.g.
  it stops furnaces from melting in the manufacture of steel.

(see page 118)

Supplement
Problems of supply

Millions of people die each year from waterborne diseases, such as typhoid and cholera, because the water they drink is contaminated with microorganisms.

Crops will not grow without an adequate supply of water – they need irrigating. Without water they die and thousands starve.

Quick test
1. State **one** chemical test for water.
2. Name the process by which undissolved solids are removed from the water supply during treatment.
3. Explain why chlorine is added to drinking water.
4. State **two** uses of water in industry.

Supplement
5. State **two** reasons why thousands of people can die during droughts.

Clean, dry air is composed of approximately:

- 78% nitrogen
- 21% oxygen
- 1% noble gases and carbon dioxide.

Supplement

Separating nitrogen and oxygen from liquid air

Fractional distillation is used to separate nitrogen and oxygen from liquid air:

1. As air is cooled, water vapour condenses and carbon dioxide freezes. They are removed.
2. Liquid air passes into a fractionating column, where the bottom is warmer than the top.
3. Nitrogen boils as the liquid air warms up and nitrogen gas is removed at the top of the column.
4. Liquid oxygen is removed at the bottom of the column.

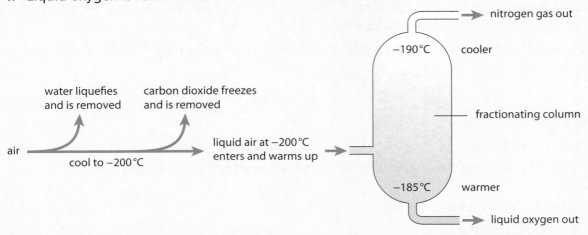

> ### Revision tip
>
> Remember, fractional distillation can be used to separate mixtures of liquids because of their different boiling points (see page 11) and the fractional distillation of petroleum (see page 124).

Common pollutants in the air

The table shows the main sources and adverse effects of common air pollutants.

Pollutant	Source	Adverse effect
carbon monoxide, CO	**incomplete combustion** of carbon-containing substances, such as fossil fuels like petrol and methane	• a poisonous gas, which stops the blood from carrying oxygen
sulfur dioxide, SO_2	combustion of fossil fuels that contain sulfur compounds	• forms acid rain, which corrodes stonework containing calcium carbonate • causes breathing difficulties
oxides of nitrogen, NO_x, e.g. NO and NO_2	car engines	• NO_2 forms acid rain, which corrodes stonework containing calcium carbonate • causes breathing difficulties
lead compounds	burning leaded petrol	• it is toxic and can cause brain and nerve damage

Oxides of nitrogen, NO_x, are formed in car engines and removed by catalytic converters.

Nitrogen, N_2, has a triple covalent bond holding the two nitrogen atoms together, $N\equiv N$ (see page 118).

The triple bond makes nitrogen very unreactive, so it exists in the atmosphere without reacting with oxygen.

Car engines reach very high temperatures. The triple bond breaks and nitrogen oxides are formed:

nitrogen + oxygen → nitrogen monoxide

$$N_2(g) + O_2(g) \rightarrow 2NO(g)$$

Nitrogen dioxide can also be formed.

NO_x is often used to show that there is more than one oxide of nitrogen formed.

Nitrogen oxides cause breathing difficulties and, in towns and cities, they can rise to dangerous levels.

Catalytic converters in car exhaust systems remove nitrogen oxides as non-toxic nitrogen. The catalyst used is platinum, which is coated onto a honeycomb mesh of silicon dioxide to increase its surface area and speed up the rate of reaction:

$$2NO_x(g) \rightarrow N_2(g) + xO_2(g)$$

Revision tip

Remember, loss of oxygen is called **reduction**, so nitrogen oxides are *reduced* to nitrogen (see page 70).

Quick test

1. State the gas that is present in the largest proportion in clean, dry air.
2. Name the pollutant gas formed when petrol combusts incompletely.
3. Explain how sulfur dioxide is formed when fossil fuels are burned.
4. Name **two** gases that can form acid rain.

Supplement

5. Explain how nitrogen oxides are formed in car engines and give the balanced equation for the formation of nitrogen dioxide.

Earth's atmosphere and climate change

Carbon dioxide, CO_2, and methane, CH_4, are **greenhouse gases**.

When the Sun warms the Earth, the planet radiates heat into the atmosphere and most of this heat is then lost into space.

Greenhouse gases trap the heat and the atmosphere warms up.

Some greenhouse gases are needed in the atmosphere to stop the planet getting too cold. However, if the proportion of greenhouse gases in the atmosphere increases too much, they could give rise to global warming.

Many scientists think that global warming is causing Earth's climate to change.

Sources of carbon dioxide and methane

Greenhouse gas	Source
carbon dioxide	• **complete combustion** of carbon-containing substances, e.g. burning fossil fuels like coal, petrol and natural gas (methane): methane + oxygen → carbon dioxide + water $CH_4(g) + 2O_2(g) \rightarrow CO_2(g) + 2H_2O(l)$ • respiration by plants and animals produces CO_2
methane	• decomposing plant matter where there is no oxygen • waste gas from digestion in animals, particularly cows

> ### Revision tip
>
> Remember, carbon dioxide is formed in the lab by adding acids to carbonates (see page 77):
>   carbonate + acid → salt + water + carbon dioxide
> It is also formed by the thermal decomposition of carbonates (see page 87):
>   metal carbonate $\xrightarrow{heat}$ metal oxide + carbon dioxide

Supplement
The carbon cycle
The amount of carbon dioxide in the atmosphere is kept fairly constant due to three key processes. These are linked in the **carbon cycle**:

1. **Photosynthesis** removes carbon dioxide from the atmosphere using the energy from sunlight to make carbon-containing compounds. The process also produces oxygen.

    carbon dioxide + water → glucose + oxygen

2. **Respiration** returns carbon dioxide to the atmosphere. Remember that animals, plants and microorganisms all respire.

    glucose + oxygen → carbon dioxide + water. This is an exothermic reaction.

3. **Combustion** also returns carbon dioxide to the atmosphere. When any carbon-containing substance burns completely, carbon dioxide is produced, e.g. octane in petrol:

    $C_8H_{18}(l) + 12.5O_2(g) \rightarrow 8CO_2(g) + 9H_2O(l)$

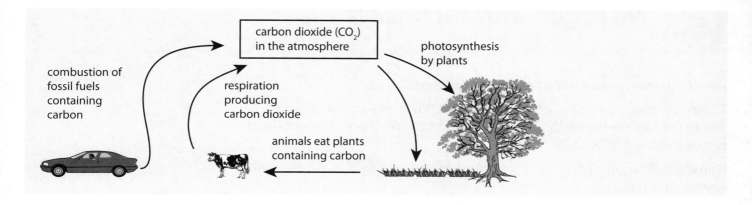

Quick test

1. Explain why methane and carbon dioxide are called greenhouse gasses.
2. State the name of the process by which every living organism produces carbon dioxide.
3. Which greenhouse gas is produced by the complete combustion of fossil fuels?
4. Which greenhouse gas is produced from decomposing plant matter?

Supplement

5. Name the process that removes carbon dioxide from the atmosphere.

Nitrogen and fertilisers

Living organisms need nitrogen to make proteins.

The atmosphere contains 78% nitrogen, but it is a very unreactive gas and cannot be used directly. This is due to the strong triple covalent bond between atoms of nitrogen, $N\equiv N$.

Plants get their nitrogen from compounds in the soil, such as nitrates and ammonium salts.

NPK fertilisers

Nitrogen compounds in the soil can easily get used up by plants and so they need replacing.

Plants require other elements too for healthy growth and to produce good crop yields. Two of the most important are phosphorus and potassium.

Artificial fertilisers often include all three elements: nitrogen, N, phosphorus, P, and potassium, K. This is why they are called NPK fertilisers.

Fertiliser	Formula	Essential elements
ammonium nitrate	NH_4NO_3	nitrogen
ammonium phosphate	$(NH_4)_3PO_4$	nitrogen and phosphorus
ammonium sulfate	$(NH_4)_2SO_4$	nitrogen
potassium nitrate	KNO_3	potassium and nitrogen

Supplement
Manufacturing ammonia by the Haber process

Ammonia is an important chemical used in the manufacture of most nitrogen-containing fertilisers.

The **Haber process** was invented by the German chemist, Fritz Haber:

nitrogen + hydrogen $\rightleftharpoons$ ammonia
$$N_2(g) \;+\; 3H_2(g) \;\rightleftharpoons\; 2NH_3(g)$$

Nitrogen is obtained from air (see page 114).

There are two sources of hydrogen: the **cracking** of hydrocarbons (see page 125) or the reaction of natural gas with steam.

The reaction used in the Haber process is reversible, as shown by $\rightleftharpoons$. This means it can go in both directions and the reaction could reach equilibrium in a closed system.

> **Revision tip**
>
> How the conditions for this process affect the position of equilibrium and the rate is explained on page 69.

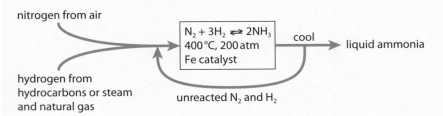

Conditions for the Haber process are chosen to obtain maximum yield at the fastest rate:

Pressure: 200 atmospheres

Increasing the pressure shifts the equilibrium to the side with fewest moles.

In this reaction, there are four moles of reactants ($N_2 + 3H_2$) and only two moles of product ($2NH_3$), so increasing the pressure shifts the equilibrium to the right to produce more ammonia.

Temperature: 400 °C

Increasing the temperature will shift the equilibrium in the direction of the endothermic reaction. Decreasing the temperature will shift the equilibrium in the exothermic direction.

This reaction is exothermic, so a low temperature will shift the equilibrium to the right to increase the yield of ammonia.

However, a low temperature gives a very slow rate of reaction, so 400 °C is a compromise to get a reasonable yield of ammonia with a reasonable rate of reaction.

Iron catalyst

An iron catalyst increases the rate of both the forward and reverse reaction, so the equilibrium is achieved faster. It does not affect the position of the equilibrium.

After the gases have passed over the catalyst, ammonia is separated by cooling and liquefying, while unreacted nitrogen and hydrogen are recycled back onto the catalyst.

Revision tip

How reaction conditions affect the Contact process is explained on page 106. You should learn the conditions for both of these manufacturing processes

Quick test

1. Explain why all living things need the element nitrogen.
2. Explain why plants cannot use nitrogen directly from the atmosphere.
3. Name the **three** essential elements provided by NPK fertilisers.
4. Explain why the compound urea, $CO(NH_2)_2$, could be used as a fertiliser.

Supplement

5. List **three** important conditions required in the Haber process and give the balanced equation for this reaction.

Exam-style practice questions

1 The apparatus set-up below was used to test the products produced when methane from natural gas was burned in a Bunsen burner flame.

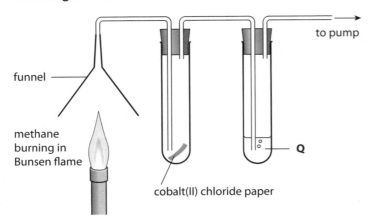

(a) The cobalt(II) chloride paper was blue.

   (i) What change would be observed after a few minutes of drawing the air from above the Bunsen flame through the apparatus? [1]

   (ii) Use your answer to part (i) to suggest the identity of one of the products formed from burning methane. [1]

(b) Carbon dioxide is also a product.

   Name the solution **Q** in the second test tube that is used to test for this gas and state the changes that would be observed. [2]

(c) Carbon dioxide and methane are greenhouse gases.

   (i) Explain what is meant by the term 'greenhouse gas'. [1]

   (ii) State **two** main sources of methane in the atmosphere. [2]

2 A student sets up the apparatus shown to investigate the volume of oxygen in a clean, dry sample of air.

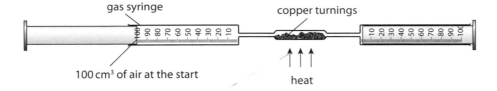

The student starts to heat the copper turnings and pushes the air back and forth over the heated copper. The volume of air in the apparatus decreases.

(a) What colour change is observed as the copper reacts? [1]

(b) Compete the equation:

   ....$Cu(s)$ + ...(g) → ....$CuO(s)$ [1]

(c) There is still unreacted copper left in the heated tube when there is no further decrease in volume of the air in the syringe.

(i) Predict the final volume of air in the syringe and explain your reasons. [2]

(ii) In this experiment copper is in excess.

Explain what would happen to the final volume of air in the syringe if there was too little copper in the heated tube. [2]

Supplement

3 Nitrogen and oxygen can be separated from liquid air using the industrial apparatus below.

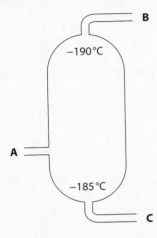

Some data about carbon dioxide, nitrogen and oxygen is shown below:

Substance	Melting point / °C	Boiling point / °C
nitrogen	−210	−196
oxygen	−219	−183

Carbon dioxide has a sublimation point of −79 °C.

(a) What is the change of state of carbon dioxide as air is cooled to −79 °C at room pressure? [1]

(b) Carbon dioxide is removed from the air and the remaining gases cooled to −200 °C to form liquid air.

(i) State the name of the process by which oxygen and nitrogen are separated. [1]

(ii) Suggest a name for the industrial apparatus. [1]

(iii) At which point, **A**, **B** or **C**, does liquid air enter the apparatus? [1]

(iv) At which point, **A**, **B** or **C**, does oxygen leave the apparatus?

Explain your reasons. [2]

(v) At which point, **A**, **B** or **C**, does nitrogen leave the apparatus?

Explain your reasons. [2]

4   The composition of car exhaust emissions is shown in the table:

Gas	Percentage in car exhaust emissions
gas X	72.0
carbon dioxide	14.0
water vapour	13.0
carbon monoxide	2.6
nitrogen oxides	0.2
hydrocarbons	0.2
sulfur dioxide	less than 0.0003

(a) Suggest the name of gas X.   [1]

(b) Heptane, C_7H_{16}, is one of the compounds found in petrol.

Complete this equation to show the complete combustion of heptane. State symbols are not required.

C_7H_{16} + ... → ....CO_2 + ...   [3]

(c) Explain why carbon monoxide is present in car exhaust emissions.   [1]

(d) State the adverse effect on health of high levels of carbon monoxide in air.   [1]

(e) Sulfur dioxide is only found in tiny amounts in car exhaust emissions.

  (i) State the main source of sulfur dioxide in the atmosphere.   [1]

  (ii) State the adverse effect on health of high levels of sulfur dioxide in air.   [1]

  (iii) Explain why sulfur dioxide in the air damages buildings made of stone containing calcium carbonate.   [1]

(f) In most countries of the world, lead compounds in petrol have been banned.

Describe an adverse health effect caused by lead compounds polluting the air?   [1]

(g) Carbon dioxide is a major product in car exhaust emissions.

Explain why many scientists are very concerned about this.   [2]

(h) Other pollutants that cause serious health problems are nitrogen oxides.

  (i) State a health problem nitrogen oxides cause.   [1]

Supplement

  (ii) Explain how nitrogen oxides form in car engines. Include one equation in your answer.   [3]

  (iii) Car exhaust emissions contain much smaller amounts of nitrogen oxides than are formed in car engines.

Explain how nitrogen oxides are removed and include an equation.   [2]

5 Water supplies are treated to make them safe to drink.

(a) Untreated water is passed through gravel beds.

Explain why this is done. [1]

(b) A small amount of chlorine is added to water before it is released into drinking supplies.

Explain the purpose of adding chlorine. [1]

(c) State **one** use of water in industry. [1]

(d) Describe a test for chlorine gas. [2]

Supplement

6 The processes in the table form part of the carbon cycle.

Complete the table to show the gas that is removed from the atmosphere by each process and the gas that is returned to the atmosphere.

Process	Gas removed from the atmosphere	Gas returned to the atmosphere
combustion		
respiration		
photosynthesis		

[2]

7 Many farmers add artificial fertilisers to the soil.

(a) What is meant by the term *fertiliser*? [1]

(b) Name **two** essential elements that plants require for healthy growth other than nitrogen. [2]

(c) Ammonium sulfate, $(NH_4)_2SO_4$, is used as an artificial fertiliser.

To make this compound ammonia is reacted with another compound.

State the name of this compound. [1]

Supplement

(d) Calculate the percentage of nitrogen in ammonium sulfate.

(A_r of N = 14, H = 1, O = 16 and S = 32) [2]

(e) The Haber process manufactures ammonia.

(i) Write the chemical equation for this reaction. [1]

(ii) List the essential conditions used in the Haber process.

You need not refer to rate or yield in your answer. [3]

Fuels

Organic chemistry is the chemistry of carbon compounds.

These were originally thought to be associated with living organisms. However, today, organic chemistry covers millions of chemicals from plastics to fuels. It does not include metal carbonates and metal hydrogen carbonates, which are inorganic chemicals.

Fuels

Fuels release heat energy when they combust (burn) in oxygen. This energy released can be used to do work, such as generate electricity or move a car.

Three of the most important fuels are coal, natural gas and petroleum. These are called **fossil fuels** because they were formed over millions of years from dead plants and animals:

- Coal is mainly carbon.
- Natural gas is mainly methane, CH_4.
- Petroleum is a mixture of hydrocarbons.

These fuels are also **non-renewable**, which means that once they have been used they will run out.

If these fuels completely combust in air, one of the products is carbon dioxide, which is a greenhouse gas linked to climate change.

Chemists play a crucial role in seeking alternative sources of energy to fossil fuels.

Revision tip

You can read more about fuels and energy transfer on page 58.

Revision tip

Petroleum is the word the syllabus uses for the crude oil that is extracted from the ground.

Fractional distillation of petroleum

Hydrocarbons are molecules containing carbon and hydrogen atoms only.

Petroleum is separated into hydrocarbon **fractions** by **fractional distillation**.

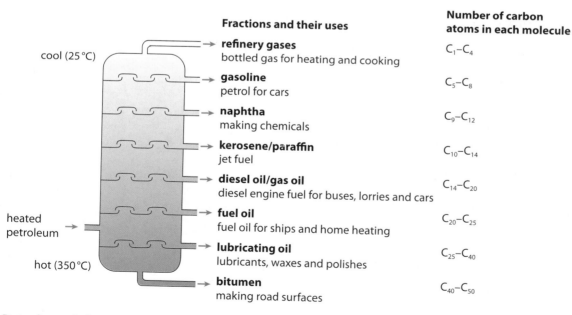

Fractions and their uses	Number of carbon atoms in each molecule
refinery gases bottled gas for heating and cooking	C_1–C_4
gasoline petrol for cars	C_5–C_8
naphtha making chemicals	C_9–C_{12}
kerosene/paraffin jet fuel	C_{10}–C_{14}
diesel oil/gas oil diesel engine fuel for buses, lorries and cars	C_{14}–C_{20}
fuel oil fuel oil for ships and home heating	C_{20}–C_{25}
lubricating oil lubricants, waxes and polishes	C_{25}–C_{40}
bitumen making road surfaces	C_{40}–C_{50}

cool (25 °C)

heated petroleum

hot (350 °C)

Petroleum is heated in a furnace to 350 °C and enters the fractionating column. The hydrocarbons separate into fractions that contain compounds with similar boiling points.

The fractionating column is coolest at the top. The lower the boiling point of the compounds, the further they travel up the column as gases before condensing.

Hydrocarbons with the smallest molecules, such as propane, C_3H_8, and butane, C_4H_{10}, rise to the very top and stay as gases.

Most of the fractions are liquids and are drawn off in the middle of the column.

The largest molecules in petroleum separate as solids and are drawn off at the bottom of the column. This is called the bitumen fraction.

Going up the column the molecules:

- have fewer carbon atoms
- are less viscous (sticky) and flow more easily
- have lower boiling points
- are more flammable (ignite more easily).

Revision tip

Make sure you know the order in which the fractions come off from the column and a use for each of them. Also, remember the properties of the molecules within a fraction, such as boiling point, viscosity and flammability.

Cracking

There is not as much demand for large hydrocarbon molecules because they are less useful than smaller hydrocarbons. They are too viscous and they do not catch fire easily.

Cracking is usually carried out by heating the large hydrocarbon molecules and passing the vapour over a catalyst, e.g.

$$decane \xrightarrow[\text{catalyst}]{\text{heat}} octane + ethene$$

$$C_{10}H_{22} \xrightarrow[\text{catalyst}]{\text{heat}} C_8H_{18} + C_2H_4$$

Definition

Cracking is the breaking down of larger hydrocarbon molecules into smaller, more useful hydrocarbon molecules.

This is an example of just one cracking reaction. The chain in the larger hydrocarbon can break anywhere, so many smaller hydrocarbon molecules can be produced.

Hydrogen is also an important by-product of cracking. Much of the hydrogen produced is used in the Haber process to manufacture ammonia (see page 118).

Revision tip

Notice that the alkene, ethene, has a double bond, which makes this molecule reactive and very useful for making other organic molecules (see page 129).

Quick test

1. Name **three** fossil fuels.
2. Explain what is meant by the terms **(a)** hydrocarbon and **(b)** fraction.
3. State the main use of the naphtha fraction.
4. State **two** differences in the properties of the molecules in the gasoline fraction and the diesel oil fraction.
5. Decane can be cracked in a reaction to give two hydrocarbons, one of which has a molecular formula C_6H_{14}. Deduce the molecular formula of the other compound.

Alkanes

Alkanes:

- are **saturated hydrocarbons** – all the carbon atoms in their molecules are joined by single bonds only
- are a **homologous series** – they are a family of similar compounds, with similar chemical properties
- do not have a **functional group** – they only have strong C–C and C–H bonds in their molecules.

Alkane	Molecular formula	Structural formula	Structure showing all atoms and bonds
methane	CH_4	CH_4	
ethane	C_2H_6	CH_3CH_3	
propane	C_3H_8	$CH_3CH_2CH_3$	
butane	C_4H_{10}	$CH_3CH_2CH_2CH_3$	

- All the names end in –*ane*.
- *meth*– means there is one carbon atom in the molecule.
- *eth*– means there are two carbon atoms in the molecule joined in a chain.
- *prop*– and *but*– mean there are three and four carbon atoms respectively, joined in a chain.
- The lines between the C and H atoms represent single covalent bonds.

Supplement

The characteristics of the compounds in a homologous series:

- They have the same general formula. The general formula for alkanes is C_nH_{2n+2}, where *n* is the number of carbon atoms.
- Each member differs from the next by a CH_2 group.
- There is a gradual change in their physical properties, e.g. melting points and boiling points steadily increase as the number of carbon atoms increase. This is due to an increase in the relative molecular mass, M_r, and length of the molecules.
- They have similar chemical properties because they have the same functional group. It is the functional group that determines the chemical properties of molecules.

Alkanes are one of the only homologous series that do not have a functional group. However, they still have similar chemical properties because they only contain C–H and C–C bonds.

Structural isomerism

Carbon always has four covalent bonds in organic compounds. Hydrogen forms only one bond.

This means that for methane, ethane and propane there is only one way to arrange the atoms in their molecules. It is different for butane – butane has a **structural isomer**.

Definition
Structural isomers are molecules with the same molecular formula but different structural formulae.

Butane and methylpropane show structural isomerism:

Alkane	Molecular formula	Structure showing all atoms and bonds
butane	C_4H_{10}	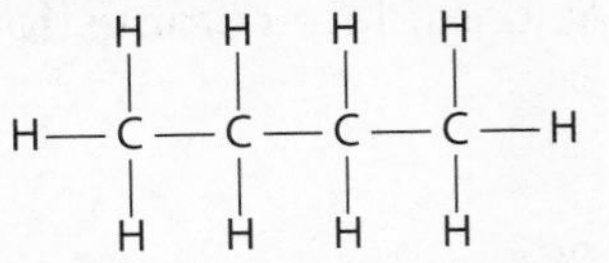
methylpropane	C_4H_{10}	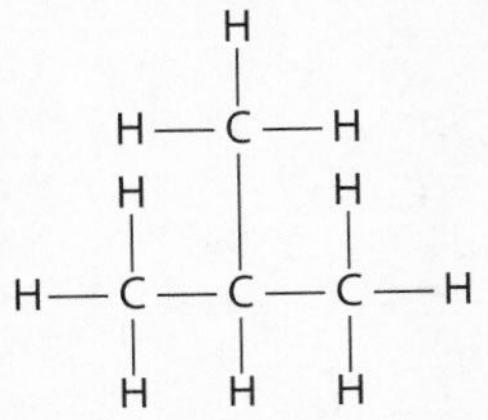

Both molecules have the same molecular formulae, C_4H_{10}, but their structural formulae are different.

> **Revision tip**
>
> The structures shown in both tables for this topic are structural formulae.

Chemical properties of alkanes

Alkanes are generally unreactive, partly because the C–H and C–C covalent bonds are strong and take a lot of energy to break. However, they do burn in air and oxygen.

With a plentiful supply of air, alkanes undergo **complete combustion** to form carbon dioxide and water, e.g.

methane + oxygen → carbon dioxide + water
$$CH_4(g) + 2O_2(g) \rightarrow CO_2(g) + 2H_2O(l)$$

Alkanes are used as fuels because they release a lot of heat energy when they burn, which can be used to do work.

In a limited supply of air or oxygen, **incomplete combustion** takes place and carbon monoxide forms, which is poisonous.

> **Revision tip**
>
> Carbon monoxide is one of the pollutants from car engines (see page 114). It is a poisonous gas that stops the blood from carrying oxygen.

Supplement

Substitution reactions with chlorine

A **substitution reaction** is when one atom is swapped for another.

Methane reacts with chlorine in the presence of ultraviolet light. A hydrogen atom is substituted for a chlorine atom:

methane + chlorine → chloromethane + hydrogen chloride

$$CH_4(g) + Cl_2(g) \rightarrow CH_3Cl(l) + HCl(g)$$

Other substitution reactions are possible if there is too much chlorine – CH_2Cl_2, $CHCl_3$ and CCl_4 can all be formed.

Revision tip

This reaction is **photochemical reaction**. For other photochemical reactions see page 66.

Quick test

1. Describe what is meant by the term *homologous series*.
2. Name the molecule with a molecular formula C_2H_6 and draw its structure. Show all atoms and bonds.
3. State the name of the type of bond present in alkane molecules.
4. Write the word and balanced equations for the complete combustion of ethane.

Supplement

5. **(a)** Write the molecular formula of these alkanes.

6. Write the balanced equation for the reaction of ethane with chlorine and state the condition required.

(b) Explain why these molecules are structural isomers.

6. Write the balanced equation for the reaction of ethane with chlorine and state the condition required.

Alkenes:

- are **unsaturated hydrocarbons** – they contain a C=C double bond and their molecules are made up of carbon and hydrogen atoms only
- are a **homologous series** of compounds with similar chemical properties due to the alkene **functional group**, the C=C double bond, which makes them more reactive compounds than the alkanes
- are manufactured by cracking larger hydrocarbon molecules using heat and a catalyst (see page 125). Hydrogen can also be produced in this process, e.g.

$$C_{10}H_{22} \xrightarrow[\text{catalyst}]{\text{heat}} C_6H_{12} + 2C_2H_4 + H_2$$

> **Revision tip**
>
> A large hydrocarbon molecule can crack in many different ways to produce many different combinations of products. Always check that the total number of carbon atoms and the total number of hydrogen atoms on each side of the equation are the same.

Alkene	Molecular formula	Structural formula	Structure showing all atoms and bonds
ethene	C_2H_4	$CH_2{=}CH_2$	H H C=C H H
propene	C_3H_6	$CH_3CH{=}CH_2$	H H H—C—C=C H H H
but-1-ene	C_4H_8	$CH_3CH_2CH{=}CH_2$	H H H H—C—C—C=C H H H H
but-2-ene		$CH_3CH{=}CHCH_3$	H H H H H—C—C=C—C—H H H

> **Revision tip**
>
> - If you are following the Core syllabus, you need only remember how to name and draw the structure of ethene. If you are studying the Supplement, you should practise naming and drawing all four alkenes.
> - When drawing organic structures, remember that each carbon always has four bonds attached to other atoms and hydrogen has one single bond.

- All the names end in *–ene*.
- *Eth–*, *prop–* and *but–* tell you the number of carbon atoms bonded together in a chain in the molecule.

Test to distinguish between saturated and unsaturated hydrocarbons

Unsaturated hydrocarbons, such as alkenes, turn aqueous bromine from orange to colourless. This is a test for C=C double bonds.

Alkanes are saturated hydrocarbons and the orange colour of aqueous bromine does not change.

Supplement

The general formula of the alkenes is C_nH_{2n}, where *n* is the number of carbon atoms.

Just as with the alkanes, there is a gradual increase in melting points and boiling points as the number of carbon atoms in the molecules increases.

Structural isomerism

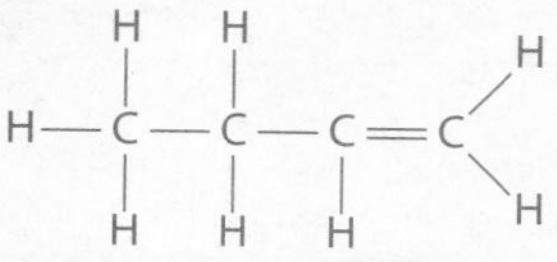

but-1-ene

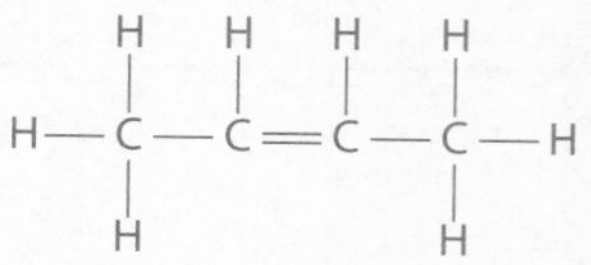

but-2-ene

These butene molecules are structural isomers – they have the same molecular formula, C_4H_8, but different structural formulae.

The -1- and the -2- in these names show that the double bond is attached to the first or second carbon in the molecule.

Chemical properties of alkenes

The C=C double bond makes alkenes reactive. The test for this bond is aqueous bromine – it turns from orange to colourless.

Supplement
Addition reactions

> **Definition**
>
> An **addition reaction** is when two molecules react together to form one larger molecule with no other products.

In addition reactions, the double bond in an alkene breaks and molecules add across it.

Addition reaction with bromine
The test for a C=C double bond is aqueous bromine – it is decolourised.

This is an addition reaction:

ethene	+	bromine	→	1,2-dibromoethane
(colourless gas)		(orange in aqueous solution)		(colourless liquid)
C_2H_4	+	Br_2	→	CH_2BrCH_2Br

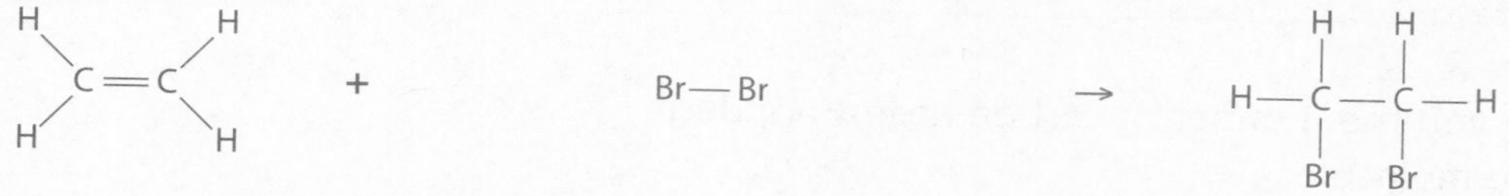

Addition reaction with hydrogen
Ethene is heated with a nickel catalyst to form ethane:

ethene	+	hydrogen	→	ethane
C_2H_4	+	H_2	→	CH_3CH_3

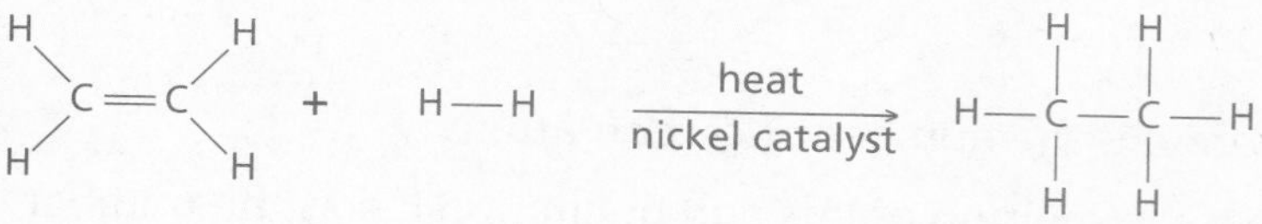

Addition reaction with steam

Ethanol is formed in this important reaction. High temperature and high pressure are used together with a phosphoric acid catalyst:

ethene	+	steam	$\rightarrow$	ethanol
C_2H_4	+	H_2O	$\rightarrow$	C_2H_5OH

This reaction is used to manufacture ethanol (see page 133).

Formation of poly(ethene)

Poly(ethene) is also called polythene. It is a **polymer**.

> **Definition**
>
> **Polymers** are large molecules built up from small units called **monomers**.

The monomer in poly(ethene) is ethene.

This equation below shows just three ethene monomers joining together to form a small part of the polymer chain. In practice, many thousands of ethene monomers join together to form one very large molecule.

ethene monomers   part of a very large poly(ethene) molecule

This type of reaction is called **addition polymerisation**.

> **Definition**
>
> During **addition polymerisation**, all the monomers join together to form the polymer and there are no other products.

This addition polymerisation reaction is often shown like this, where n is a very large number.

repeat unit

The polymer is such a large molecule that only the **repeat unit** is shown, i.e. the smallest complete unit from which the molecule is made.

The ethene repeat unit is enclosed in brackets. Notice that the bonds at each end of the polymer go through the brackets to show that it is part of a very long chain of monomers joined together.

Quick test

1. Explain why alkenes are called *unsaturated hydrocarbons*.
2. State the molecular formula and draw the structural formula of ethene showing all atoms and bonds.
3. Explain what is meant by the term *polymerisation*.
4. Using *n* to represent a large number, give the equation for the formation of poly(ethene).

Supplement

5. Write a balanced equation for the reaction of propene with hydrogen and name the product formed.

Alcohols form another homologous series of compounds. The compounds all have similar chemical properties because they contain the alcohol functional group, –OH. The names of all the members of this homologous series end in –ol. The most well-known member of this family of compounds is ethanol, C_2H_5OH.

Alcohol	Formula	Structural formula	Structure showing all atoms and bonds
methanol	CH_3OH	CH_3OH	H—C—O—H (with H above and below C)
ethanol	C_2H_5OH	CH_3CH_2OH	H—C—C—O—H
propan-1-ol	C_3H_7OH	$CH_3CH_2CH_2OH$	H—C—C—C—O—H
butan-1-ol	C_4H_9OH	$CH_3CH_2CH_2CH_2OH$	H—C—C—C—C—O—H

> **Revision tip**
>
> If you are following the Core syllabus, you need only remember how to name and draw the structure of ethanol. If you are studying the Supplement, you should practise naming and drawing all four alcohols.

Supplement

The general formula of the alcohols is $C_nH_{2n+1}OH$.

Just as with any homologous series, there is a gradual increase in melting points and boiling points as the number of carbon atoms in the molecules increases.

Structural isomerism

These two molecules are structural isomers because they have the same molecular formula, C_3H_7OH, but different structural formulae.

The -1- and -2- show which carbon atom the –OH group is bonded to.

propan-1-ol   propan-2-ol

The manufacture of ethanol

There are two main methods of manufacturing ethanol.

During **fermentation**, the enzymes in yeast catalyse the breakdown of sugar in aqueous solution to form ethanol:

glucose $\xrightarrow[\text{37 °C, no oxygen}]{\text{enzymes in yeast}}$ ethanol + carbon dioxide

$C_6H_{12}O_6 \xrightarrow[\text{37 °C, no oxygen}]{\text{enzymes in yeast}} 2C_2H_5OH + 2CO_2$

> **Revision tip**
>
> Enzymes are biological catalysts that speed up the rate of reactions (see page 64).

Yeast is a living organism and its enzymes work best at around human body temperature (37 °C).

Yeast cannot survive when the concentration of ethanol is too high. When the concentration of ethanol in the fermenting solution reaches about 15%, the yeast starts to die and no more ethanol is produced.

To separate the dead yeast from the solution, the mixture is **filtered**.

To separate the ethanol from the water in the solution, **fractional distillation** is used (see page 12).

Ethanol can be used as a fuel. If it is manufactured by fermentation, it is a **renewable fuel** because the glucose used is obtained from plants.

Catalytic addition of steam
In this method of manufacturing ethanol, steam (water) adds across the double bond:

Revision tip

Remember, in an addition reaction, two molecules react together to form one larger molecule with no other products.

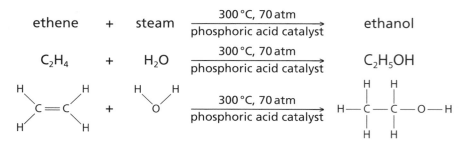

The ethene for this process is obtained from the cracking of large alkane molecules found in petroleum fractions (see page 125).

Supplement

Advantages and disadvantages of the two methods of manufacturing ethanol
The table below compares the two methods of ethanol manufacture:

Feature of process	Fermentation	Catalytic addition of steam
raw material	glucose comes from plants, so is renewable	ethene comes from petroleum, so is non-renewable
conditions	• 37 °C and atmospheric pressure (1 atm) • little energy required except to harvest and transport the crops	• 300 °C and 70 atm • both conditions require a lot of energy, which is probably provided by burning fossil fuels
type of process	batch process, which means that the process must be stopped and restarted – this takes time and increases the cost of the process	continuous process, which means that it can be kept going day and night so long as the raw materials are present
rate of reaction	slow	fast
percentage yield	low – about 15% the ethanol must be separated from the water by fractional distillation – this requires energy, often from burning fossil fuels	very high – almost 100%

Properties and uses of ethanol

Combustion

Ethanol burns in air or oxygen. The equation for its complete combustion is:

$$\text{ethanol} + \text{oxygen} \rightarrow \text{carbon dioxide} + \text{water}$$
$$C_2H_5OH + 3O_2 \rightarrow 2CO_2 + 3H_2O$$

Revision tip

Practise balancing equations. Close this book and try and balance this equation. Remember, when balancing the number of O atoms, ethanol also contains an O atom.

Uses of ethanol

Ethanol can be used as:

* a fuel – when it burns, it gives out a lot of energy so it is a good fuel and, if it is made from plant sugars, it is also a renewable fuel
* a solvent – the –OH group in the ethanol molecule allows ethanol to dissolve many organic **compounds**. It also dissolves in water. Ethanol is used as a solvent in perfumes and disinfectants.

Supplement

Oxidising ethanol to form ethanoic acid

Ethanol can be oxidised to form ethanoic acid, CH_3COOH, a carboxylic acid.

Revision tip

The next topic tells you more about carboxylic acids.

There are two ways of oxidising ethanol:

* using oxygen from air:
$$\text{ethanol} + \text{oxygen} \rightarrow \text{ethanoic acid} + \text{water}$$
$$C_2H_5OH + O_2 \rightarrow CH_3COOH + H_2O$$
This can happen in the fermentation process if air is allowed in.
* using acidified potassium manganate(VII), $KMnO_4(aq)$:
$$C_2H_5OH + 2[O] \rightarrow CH_3COOH + H_2O$$
The [O] shows that the oxygen has come from an oxidising agent.

Revision tip

Acidified potassium manganate(VII) is a powerful oxidising agent and changes from a purple solution to a colourless solution (see page 86).

Making esters

Esters are made when a carboxylic acid reacts with an alcohol, e.g.

$$\text{ethanoic acid} + \text{ethanol} \xrightarrow{\text{conc. } H_2SO_4 \text{ catalyst}} \text{ethyl ethanoate} + \text{water}$$
$$CH_3COOH + C_2H_5OH \xrightarrow{\text{conc. } H_2SO_4 \text{ catalyst}} CH_3COOC_2H_5 + H_2O$$

This is covered in more detail in the next topic.

Quick test

1. Draw the structure of ethanol showing all atoms and bonds.
2. State the conditions required for the manufacture of ethanol by fermentation.
3. Give the word and balanced equation for the manufacture of ethanol from ethene and steam.
4. Name **two** uses of ethanol.

Supplement

5. State the general formula for the alcohols.
6. Give **one** advantage and **one** disadvantage of manufacturing ethanol by fermentation.

Carboxylic acids

Carboxylic acids form another homologous series of compounds. All the compounds have similar chemical properties because they contain the carboxylic acid functional group, –COOH.

The names of all the members of this homologous series end in –*oic acid*.

The most well-known of the carboxylic acids is ethanoic acid, CH_3COOH.

Ethanoic acid can be made by oxidation of ethanol. This can be during the fermentation process, when air is allowed in, or by using the oxidising agent acidified potassium manganate(VII) (see page 86).

Pure ethanoic acid is a liquid with a very pungent smell. When it dissolves in water it forms an aqueous solution. This solution can be called vinegar.

Carboxylic acid	Formula	Structural formula	Structure showing all atoms and bonds
methanoic acid	HCOOH	HCOOH	
ethanoic acid	CH_3COOH	CH_3COOH	
propanoic acid	C_2H_5COOH	CH_3CH_2COOH	
butanoic acid	C_3H_7COOH	$CH_3CH_2CH_2COOH$	

> **Revision tip**
>
> If you are following the Core syllabus, you need only remember how to name and draw the structure of ethanoic acid. If you are studying the Supplement, you should practise naming and drawing all four carboxylic acids.

Supplement

The general formula of the carboxylic acids is $C_nH_{2n+1}COOH$.

Just as with any homologous series, there is a gradual increase in melting points and boiling points as the number of carbon atoms in the molecules increases.

Properties of aqueous ethanoic acid

An aqueous solution of ethanoic acid behaves as a typical acid:

- It has a pH less than 7. It actually has a pH of about 4, so it is a weak acid.
- It turns litmus red and methyl orange to red.
- It reacts with metals to form a salt and hydrogen, e.g.
  ethanoic acid + magnesium → magnesium ethanoate + hydrogen
  $2CH_3COOH(aq) + Mg(s) \rightarrow (CH_3COO)_2Mg(aq) + H_2(g)$

- It reacts with bases to form a salt and water, e.g.

  ethanoic acid + sodium hydroxide → sodium ethanoate + water

  $CH_3COOH(aq) + NaOH(aq) → CH_3COONa(aq) + H_2O(l)$

Remember, sodium hydroxide is a soluble base, so it is also called an alkali.
You can read more about the properties of acids and bases in Chapter 5.

- It reacts with carbonates to form a salt, water and carbon dioxide, e.g.

  ethanoic acid + calcium carbonate → calcium ethanoate + water + carbon dioxide

  $2CH_3COOH(aq) + CaCO_3(s) → (CH_3COO)_2Ca(aq) + H_2O(l) + CO_2(g)$

Supplement

Ethanoic acid is a typical weak acid. Weak acids do not fully ionise in aqueous solutions. This means only some ethanoic acid molecules form ions:

$$CH_3COOH(aq) \rightleftharpoons CH_3COO^-(aq) + H^+(aq)$$

Although ethanoic acid shows the typical acid properties described, the reactions will be less vigorous than with strong acids, such as hydrochloric acid. This is because there is a lower concentration of hydrogen ions in aqueous ethanoic acid than there is in an aqueous solution of a strong acid of the same concentration.

Making esters

Esters are sweet-smelling compounds formed by reacting a carboxylic acid with an alcohol in the presence of concentrated sulfuric acid as a catalyst:

carboxylic acid + alcohol $\xrightarrow{\text{conc. } H_2SO_4 \text{ catalyst}}$ ester + water

For example:

propanoic acid + methanol $\xrightarrow{\text{conc. } H_2SO_4 \text{ catalyst}}$ methyl propanoate + water

> **Revision tip**
>
> The rate of reaction of magnesium with hydrochloric acid will be faster than with ethanoic acid of the same concentration. This is because there is a higher concentration of $H^+(aq)$ ions in the same volume of hydrochloric acid.
> Questions on comparing rates of reaction of strong and weak acids are frequently asked (see pages 76 and 77).

> **Revision tip**
>
> You can see the equation for the formation of ethyl ethanoate on page 135.

Quick test

1. Name this carboxylic acid:

2. Carboxylic acids form a homologous series. What is the name ending for these compounds?

3. Name the salt formed by reacting aqueous ethanoic acid with potassium hydroxide.

Supplement

4. Explain why 25 cm³ of 1 mol/dm³ nitric acid, HNO_3, reacts more quickly with magnesium than 25 cm³ of 1 mol/dm³ of aqueous ethanoic acid.

5. State the name of the ester formed from ethanol and butanoic acid and draw its structure. Show all atoms and bonds.

Polymers

Polymers are large molecules built up from small units called **monomers**.

Synthetic polymers

Petroleum is the main source of most synthetic polymers and there is a finite supply. Remember, most of the fractions in petroleum are used as fuels.

Many man-made polymers are called plastics. They can be formed into products or made into fibres to make material.

Here are some typical uses of plastics and man-made fibres:

Polymer	Use
poly(ethene)	plastic shopping bags and drinks bottles
poly(propene)	buckets, crates and ropes
poly(styrene), also called poly(phenylethene)	insulation and protective packaging
poly(chloroethene), also called PVC (polyvinyl chloride)	water pipes and insulation on electric cables
polyamide, e.g. nylon	nylon fibres are woven into fabric for clothing
polyester, e.g. *Terylene*	polyester fibres are woven into fabric for clothing

Addition polymers

The reaction to make poly(ethene) from ethene is called an **addition polymerisation** because all the monomers join together to form the polymer and there are no other products.

repeat unit

Alkenes can act as monomers because of their double bonds.

> **Revision tip**
>
> This addition polymerisation reaction is often shown like this, where n is a very large number. The brackets enclose the monomer unit and the bonds pass through these to show that this is only a very small part of a large polymer chain.

Supplement

Propene is the monomer in the formation of poly(propene).

propene   repeat unit of poly(propene)

Two more addition polymers are shown in the table:

Name of monomer	Structure of monomer	Name of polymer	Repeat unit of polymer
chloroethene		poly(chloroethene), also called PVC (polyvinyl chloride)	
tetrafluoroethene		poly(tetrafluoroethene)	

> **Revision tip**
>
> In an exam, you may be asked to deduce the structure of a polymer from a given alkene and vice versa.

Pollution problems of plastics

Plastics, like poly(ethene) and PVC, are useful because they are unreactive. This makes them **non-biodegradable**, which means they cannot be broken down by microorganisms, so disposing of them is a major problem:

- Landfill: Many plastics end up in landfill sites where they will not break down. This is a waste of a valuable material and landfill sites are filling up quickly.
- Incineration: Burning plastics often releases toxic fumes together with carbon dioxide, a greenhouse gas.
- Recycling: This saves using petroleum to make new plastics, but it can be difficult and expensive to separate the different types of plastics from household waste.

Supplement

Condensation polymers

Definition

Condensation polymers are formed when monomers join together and a small molecule is ejected.

The small molecule ejected is often water, which is why the term condensation is used for this type of polymerisation.

Revision tip

The difference between condensation polymerisation and addition polymerisation is that small molecules are ejected in condensation polymerisation. The only product formed in addition polymerisation is the polymer.

Formation of nylon

Nylon is a polyamide because the monomers are joined together by amide linkages.

Nylon is a condensation polymer and water is ejected in the process of forming it.

Formation of *Terylene*

Terylene is a polyester because the monomers are joined together by ester linkages.

It is a condensation polymer and water is ejected in the process of forming it.

Natural polymers

There are many polymers that occur in nature. Two of these are **proteins** and **carbohydrates**. Both of these natural polymers are constituents of the food we eat.

Supplement

Proteins

The monomers in proteins are **amino acids**. These are small molecules.

There are twenty different naturally occurring amino acids that can be used to make up different proteins.

In the protein structure, the boxes representing the different amino acids are shaded differently.

In protein, the amino acids are joined by amide linkages like those in nylon.

Proteins are condensation polymers because water is ejected in the process of forming them.

Proteins can be broken down into amino acids by a process known as **hydrolysis**. Hydrolysis is breaking down a compound using water:

- This is the reverse reaction to the formation of proteins shown.
- Water splits the amide linkages apart again to form the original amino acids.
- Acid is used as a catalyst.

The amino acids in a protein can be analysed by hydrolysing the protein and then using **chromatography** (see page 10) to separate the amino acids present.

> **Revision tip**
>
> Amino acids are colourless, so they are made visible on the chromatography paper by using a **locating agent**. Each amino acid has a different R_f value, which allows it to be identified.

Complex carbohydrates

Carbohydrate molecules contain carbon, hydrogen and oxygen only. Glucose, $C_6H_{12}O_6$, is a simple carbohydrate, also known as a simple sugar.

Starch is a naturally occurring condensation polymer:

- It is made up of sugar units.
- The monomers in starch and other complex carbohydrates are simple sugars.

As with proteins, starch and other complex carbohydrates can be hydrolysed to give simple sugars. This hydrolysis is the reverse of the condensation polymerisation shown:

- Water molecules split the links between the sugar units.
- Enzymes or acids catalyse this process.

The products of this hydrolysis can be separated and analysed using chromatography, in a similar way to that used to separate amino acids from the hydrolysis of proteins.

In the human body, starch is hydrolysed to provide simple sugars that are used to provide energy.

Quick test

1. Define the terms (a) *polymer* and (b) *monomer*.
2. Explain why alkenes are called *addition polymers*.
3. State a typical use for poly(ethene) and for nylon.
4. Explain why many plastics cause major pollution problems.

Supplement

5. Poly(styrene) has this repeat unit. Draw the structure of its monomer.

6. Draw the structure of part of the nylon polymer.
7. Explain what is meant by the term *condensation polymerisation*.
8. What type of linkage is common to both nylon and proteins?

Answers

Exam-style practice questions

1. (a) Ni / nickel [1]
   (b) Br / bromine [1]
   (c) Li / lithium [1]
   (d) Cl / chlorine [1]
   (e) Ar / argon [1]
   (f) Cl / chlorine (will displace bromine) [1]
2. (a) potassium hydroxide; hydrogen [2]
   (b) Any three of: fizzing / bubbles / effervescence; floats; moves; molten ball; lilac flame; solid disappears [3]
   (c) (i) Purple [1]
       (ii) pH number in the range 12–14 [1]
   (d) lithium / sodium [1]
   (e) Potassium loses an electron; to give a, full outer shell / noble gas configuration OR potassium has one electron in its outer shell; which it loses to give a full outer shell [2]
   (f) $2Li(s) + 2H_2O(l) \rightarrow 2LiOH(aq) + H_2(g)$ (correct formulae and balanced; correct state symbols) [2]
3. (a) Bromine has a lower melting point than room temperature AND a higher boiling point than room temperature [1]
   (b) Black solid [1]
   (c) Melting point value within range 210–310°C; boiling point range 290–380°C (boiling point must be above value given for melting point) [2]
   (d) Less reactive; reactivity decreases down Group VII [2]
   (e) At_2 [1]
   (f) 7 electrons [1]
   (g) 1– / At^- [1]
4. (a) Can be bent and hammered into shape [1]
   (b) Metal atoms / ions are arranged in layers; these can slide over each other [2]
   (c) An alloy is a mixture of a metal and at least one other element [1]
   (d) Carbon disrupts the layers of metal (atoms / ions); and they cannot slide over each other [2]
5. (a) Hydrogen [1]
   (b) Iron oxide (the actual compound is iron(II) oxide) [1]
   (c) iron + water → iron oxide + hydrogen [1]
   (d) $Ca(s) + 2H_2O(l) \rightarrow Ca(OH)_2(aq) + H_2(g)$ (correct formulae; equation is balanced) [2]
   (e) calcium (most reactive), iron, copper (least reactive) [1]
   (f) No change [1]

6. (a) Nickel (most reactive), tin, lead (least reactive) [1]
   (b) $Sn + PbO \rightarrow SnO + Pb$ (correct formulae; equation is balance) [2]
   (c) (i) Iron is displaced from the solution and coats the zinc strip; zinc forms, aqueous zinc ions / $Zn^{2+}(aq)$; $Zn(s) + Fe^{2+}(aq) \rightarrow Zn^{2+}(aq) + Fe(s)$ [3]
       (ii) Magnesium is more reactive than zinc; zinc cannot displace aqueous magnesium ions [2]
       (iii) Magnesium (most reactive), zinc, iron (least reactive) [1]
7. (a) Hematite [1]
   (b) (i) Limestone; coke [2]
       (ii) A [1]
       (iii) C [1]
   (c) (i) Molten slag [1]
       (ii) Molten iron [1]
   (d) $C + O_2 \rightarrow CO_2$ [1]
   (e) $CO_2 + C \rightarrow 2CO$ [1]
   (f) (i) 3, 2, 3 [1]
       (ii) Oxygen is lost [1]
   (g) (i) Carbon reacts with oxygen to form carbon dioxide; which escapes as a gas [2]
       (ii) Phosphorus(V) oxide and silicon dioxide formed; $Si(s) + O_2(g) \rightarrow SiO_2(s)$ / $4P + 5O_2 \rightarrow P_4O_{10}$ (Allow: $2P + 2.5O_2 \rightarrow P_2O_5$); these oxides are acidic (because they are non-metal oxides); they, react / are neutralised, by calcium oxide (to form slag); calcium oxide + silicon dioxide → calcium silicate / calcium oxide + phosphorus(V) oxide → calcium phosphate [4]

7 Air and water

Water

1. Add the liquid to anhydrous copper(II) sulfate. The white solid turn blue. / Add the liquid to anhydrous cobalt(II) chloride. The blue solid turns pink. The cobalt(II) chloride can be impregnated on filter paper and it turns from blue to pink.
2. Filtration (through coarse and fine gravel)
3. To kill disease-causing microorganisms
4. Any two from: solvent; raw material for the production of hydrogen; coolant to stop furnace walls from melting / decomposing
5. There is not enough drinking water; crops fail to grow, so people starve

Air

1. Nitrogen
2. Carbon monoxide
3. Fossil fuels contain sulfur compounds. When these compounds burn, they react with oxygen in the air and form sulfur dioxide.
4. Sulfur dioxide; nitrogen dioxide
5. Nitrogen reacts with oxygen because of the, high heat energy / high temperature, in a car engine. This breaks the triple bond, N≡N, in nitrogen. $N_2(g) + 2O_2(g) \rightarrow 2NO_2(g)$

Earth's atmosphere and climate change

1. They trap heat in the Earth's atmosphere
2. Respiration
3. Carbon dioxide
4. Methane
5. Photosynthesis

Nitrogen and fertilisers

1. Nitrogen is used to make proteins
2. Nitrogen is too unreactive due to the strong triple bond between nitrogen atoms
3. Nitrogen; phosphorus; potassium
4. It contains nitrogen
5. 400°C; 200 atm; iron catalyst; $N_2(g) + 3H_2(g) \rightleftharpoons 2NH_3(g)$

Exam-style practice questions

1. (a) (i) Colour change (from blue) to pink [1]
       (ii) Water is produced [1]
   (b) Limewater; turns milky [2]
   (c) (i) A greenhouse gas traps, heat / energy, in the atmosphere [1]
       (ii) Decomposing plant matter; from digestion in, animals / cows [2]
2. (a) Brown to black (both colours required) [1]
   (b) 2, O_2, 2 [1]
   (c) (i) 79 (cm³); the percentage of oxygen in clean dry air is 21% [2]
       (ii) The final volume of air would be, more / >79 cm³; because, there is an excess of oxygen / some oxygen remains unreacted [2]
3. (a) Gas to solid [1]
   (b) (i) Fractional distillation [1]
       (ii) Fractionating column / fractionating tower [1]
       (iii) A [1]
       (iv) C; oxygen is a liquid at –185°C / boiling point of oxygen is –183°C (so it falls to the bottom of the column) [2]

Answers

(v) B; nitrogen is a gas at −190 °C / boiling point of nitrogen is −196 °C [2]

4. (a) Nitrogen [1]
   (b) $C_7H_{16} + 11O_2 \rightarrow 7CO_2 + 8H_2O$ (O_2 and H_2O; 11; 7 AND 8) [3]
   (c) Incomplete combustion of petrol [1]
   (d) Poisonous because it stops the blood from carrying oxygen [1]
   (e) (i) Burning fossil fuels that contain sulfur compounds [1]
       (ii) Breathing difficulties / asthma [1]
       (iii) It forms acid rain (which reacts with calcium carbonate) [1]
   (f) Toxic / causes nerve OR brain damage [1]
   (g) CO_2 is a greenhouse gas; which traps the heat, causing the atmosphere to warm up [2]
   (h) (i) Nitrogen oxides cause breathing difficulties [1]
       (ii) At high temperatures (in car engines); nitrogen and oxygen react together; $N_2(g) + O_2(g) \rightarrow 2NO(g)$ [3]
       (iii) Catalytic converters; $2NO_x \rightarrow N_2 + xO_2$ [2]
5. (a) Filter / filtration to remove, solid / undissolved, particles [1]
   (b) To kill, microorganisms / bacteria, that could cause disease [1]
   (c) Any one from: solvent; coolant; raw material in the production of hydrogen (from methane) [1]
   (d) Bleaches; damp litmus paper [2]
6. One mark for each correctly completed column (Accept correct chemical symbols) [2]

Process	Gas removed from the atmosphere	Gas returned to the atmosphere
combustion	oxygen	carbon dioxide
respiration	oxygen	carbon dioxide
photosynthesis	carbon dioxide	oxygen

7. (a) A substance that replaces nutrients in the soil [1]
   (b) Phosphorus; potassium [2]
   (c) Sulfuric acid [1]
   (d) M_r ($(NH_4)2SO_4$): $[14 + (1 \times 4)] \times 2 + 32 + (16 \times 4)$ = 132; $\frac{28}{132} \times 100 = 21\%$ [2]
   (e) (i) $N_2(g) + 3H_2(g) \rightleftharpoons 2NH_3(g)$ [1]
       (ii) 400–500 °C; 200 atm; iron catalyst [3]

8 Organic chemistry
Fuels
1. Coal; natural gas; petroleum
2. (a) A molecule containing carbon and hydrogen atoms only
   (b) A fraction contains compounds with similar boiling points
3. To make chemicals
4. Any two from: gasoline contains fewer carbon atoms; has a lower boiling point; is more flammable; flows more easily; is less viscous than diesel oil (Accept reverse arguments)
5. C_4H_8 OR C_2H_4 (as two moles of C_2H_4 could be formed)

Alkanes
1. A family of similar compounds, with similar chemical properties due to the presence of the same functional group (Supplement: The compounds in a homologous series have the same general formula and a gradual change in physical properties. Each compound differs from the next by a CH_2 group)
2. Ethane

3. Covalent bond
4. ethane + oxygen → carbon dioxide + water; $C_2H_6 + 3.5\,O_2 \rightarrow 2CO_2 + 3H_2O$ / $2C_2H_6 + 7O_2 \rightarrow 4CO_2 + 6H_2O$
5. (a) C_5H_{12}
   (b) They have the same molecular formulae, but different structural formulae
6. $C_2H_6 + Cl_2 \rightarrow C_2H_5Cl + HCl$; condition: UV light

Alkenes
1. They are unsaturated because they contain a C=C double bond. They are hydrocarbons because their molecules contain carbon and hydrogen atoms only.
2. C_2H_4;

3. Polymerisation is when large molecules are built up from small units called monomers
4.

5. $CH_3CH=CH_2 + H_2 \rightarrow CH_3CH_2CH_3$ / $C_3H_6 + H_2 \rightarrow C_3H_8$; C_3H_8 is propane

Alcohols
1.

2. Enzymes from yeast; 37 °C; no oxygen; aqueous solution
3. ethene + steam → ethanol; $C_2H_4 + H_2O \rightarrow C_2H_5OH$
4. Fuel; solvent
5. $C_nH_{2n+1}OH$
6. Advantage: raw material comes from plants so is renewable / mild reaction conditions needed so little energy required, except to harvest and transport the crops; Disadvantage: rate of reaction is slow / percentage yield of ethanol is low and must be separated from the water by fractional distillation

Carboxylic acids
1. Ethanoic acid
2. −oic acid
3. Potassium ethanoate
4. There is lower hydrogen ion concentration in the ethanoic acid because it is a weak acid and does not fully ionise
5. Ethyl butanoate;

Polymers
1. (a) Polymers are large molecules built up from small units called monomers
   (b) Monomers are the small molecules that join together to form a polymer
2. During addition polymerisation, all the alkene monomers join together to form the polymer and there are no other products
3. Poly(ethene): plastic shopping bags / drinks bottles; nylon: fabric for clothing
4. Many plastics are non-biodegradable, so cannot be disposed of easily
5.

6.

7. Condensation polymers are formed when monomers join together and a small molecule is ejected
8. Amide linkage

Answers

Exam-style practice questions

1. (a) (i) Hydrocarbons are molecules containing <u>only</u> carbon and hydrogen atoms [1]
(ii) Fractions contain compounds with similar boiling points [1]
(b) (i) L [1]
(ii) M [1]
(iii) T [1]
(c) Any two from the following statements about R: R is more viscous / thicker / darker, longer; contains, larger molecules / molecules with more C atoms; has a higher boiling point / melting point; is less flammable (Accept reverse arguments, e.g. O is less viscous) [2]
(d) (i) naphtha [1]
(ii) fuel oil [1]
(iii) kerosene/paraffin [1]
(iv) refinery gas [1]

2. (a)

$$\begin{array}{ccc} H & & H \\ \backslash & & / \\ & C=C & \\ / & & \backslash \\ H & & H \end{array}$$
[1]

(b) Cracking (Allow: thermal decomposition) [1]
(c) butane; ethene [2]
(d) heat (Accept a given temperature in the range 450–500°C); catalyst / Al_2O_3 [2]
(e) (i) Any substituted chlorobutane product, e.g.

H—C—C—C—C—Cl
[1]
(ii) UV light [1]

3. (a)

$$\begin{array}{ccc} H & & H \\ \backslash & & / \\ & C=C & \\ / & & \backslash \\ H & & H \end{array}$$
[1]

(b) Covalent bond (Accept: double bond) [1]
(c) Alkenes [1]
(d) carbon dioxide; water [2]
(e) (i) Contains a C=C double bond [1]
(ii) Aqueous bromine; turns from orange to colourless [2]
(f) (i) C_nH_{2n} [1]
(ii) Any two from: compounds with, similar / the same, chemical properties; same functional group; a gradual increase in, melting points / boiling points, as the number of carbon atoms increases (in the molecules); a trend / pattern, in physical properties; (neighbouring members) differ by CH_2 [2]
(g) (i) C_5H_{10} [1]
(ii)

H—C—C—C—C—C—H (with Br Br on 4th and 5th carbons)
[1]
(iii) Addition reaction [1]

4. (a) (i) $2C_2H_5OH + 2CO_2$ (correct formula for C_2H_5OH; correct balancing numbers) [2]
(ii) Any two from: no oxygen; 37°C; enzymes in yeast; aqueous solution [2]
(b) (i) $H_2O + C_2H_5OH$ [2]
(ii) phosphoric acid [1]
(iii) 300°C; 70 atm [2]
(iv) Cracking (of large alkane molecules found in petroleum fractions) [1]
(c) Advantages: glucose is renewable; little energy required / temperature of 37°C [2]
Any two disadvantages from: batch process; low yield; ethanol must be separated (from water); slow rate of reaction [2]
(d) butan-1-ol and butan-2-ol (both names; correct diagram of butan-1-ol; correct diagram of butan-2-ol) [3]

H—C—C—C—C—O—H

H—C—C—C—C—H (with O H group)

5. (a) alcohol; carboxylic acid [2]
(b)

H—C—C—C (with O double bond and O—CH₃)
[1]

6. (a)

H—C—C (with =O and O—H)
[1]
(b) Any three from: it has a pH less than 7; it turns, litmus red / methyl orange to red; it reacts with metals to form a salt and hydrogen; it reacts with bases to form a salt and water; it reacts with carbonates to form a salt, water and carbon dioxide [3]
(c) A weak acid does not fully ionise in aqueous solution / Only some ethanoic acid molecules form ions [1]
(d) methanoic acid [1]
(e) propanoic acid; methanol [2]

7. (a) Many, molecules / monomers, join to form a large molecule; no other products are formed / no molecules are ejected [2]
(b)

···—C—C—C—C—···
[1]
(c) (i) Cannot be broken down; by microorganisms / microbes / bacteria [2]
(ii) Landfill sites: plastics do not, decompose / breakdown (so landfill sites fill up); Burning: toxic gases produced / carbon dioxide produced (which is a greenhouse gas) [2]

8. (a) (i)

$$n \begin{array}{c} F \quad F \\ \backslash / \\ C=C \\ / \backslash \\ F \quad F \end{array} \rightarrow \left[\begin{array}{c} F \;\; F \\ | \;\; | \\ C—C \\ | \;\; | \\ F \;\; F \end{array} \right]_n$$
[2]
(ii) Addition polymerisation [1]
(b) (i) Many monomers join together to make a large molecule; and a small molecule is ejected [2]
(ii)

H—N—■—N—H

H—O—C—■—C—O—H (with =O groups)
[2]

Glossary

Acid – a substance that dissolves in water to form $H^+(aq)$ ions. An acid is a proton donor. It has a pH less than 7.

Activation energy – the minimum energy with which particles must collide to cause a reaction.

Actual yield – the amount of a substance that is produced in a reaction. This can only be found by carrying out the reaction.

Addition polymerisation – when monomers join together to form a large molecule (polymer) and no other products are made.

Addition reaction – two molecules react together to form one larger molecule with no other products.

Alkali – a base that is soluble in water. Alkalis produce $OH^-(aq)$ ions in water.

Alkali metal – an element in Group I of the Periodic Table.

Alloy – a mixture of a metal and at least one other element.

Amount – a term used by chemists to describe the number of particles in a substance.

Amphoteric oxide – an oxide that reacts with both acids and bases to make salts and water.

Anhydrous – 'without water'. Anhydrous compounds, usually salts, do not have any water of crystallisation.

Anode – the positive electrode.

Artificial fertiliser – chemical compounds that replace nutrients in the soil, which have been used up by growing plants. NPK fertilisers contain the elements nitrogen, phosphorus and potassium, which are essential to healthy plant growth.

Atomic number (proton number) – the number of protons in the nucleus of an atom.

Avogadro constant – the number of particles (atoms, molecules or formula units) in one mole, which is 6×10^{23}.

Balanced equation – an equation in which the number of atoms of each element are the same on both sides.

Base – a substance that neutralises an acid to produce a salt and water. A base is a proton acceptor.

Basic oxygen process – this is the process for making steel using iron from the blast furnace. Oxygen is blown through molten iron and calcium oxide (a basic oxide) reacts with acidic impurities to form molten slag.

Boiling – when a liquid changes to a gas. Gas bubbles form inside the liquid and escape during boiling. This is different from evaporation, which happens below the boiling point, because the particles only escape from the liquid surface.

Boiling point – the temperature at which a liquid changes to a gas.

Bond energy – the amount of energy needed to break one mole of a particular bond.

Brownian motion – when smoke particles in air, or dust specks on a water surface, move randomly because they are being hit by particles in the air or water.

Capillary tube – a very narrow glass tube, which can be used to place small spots of liquid samples on chromatography paper.

Carbon cycle – the processes by which carbon dioxide is removed from and returned to the atmosphere.

Catalyst – a substance that increases the rate of a reaction by lowering the activation energy but is chemically unchanged at the end.

Cathode – the negative electrode.

Chromatogram – the chromatography paper showing the separated dyes or other substances, such as amino acids from the hydrolysis of proteins.

Chromatography – a process used to separate dissolved substances, such as dyes and amino acids, using chromatography paper.

Combustion – the burning of a substance in oxygen. It is a highly exothermic reaction that produces heat and often light.

Complete combustion – the burning of a substance, such as a fuel, in excess oxygen. During complete combustion of hydrocarbon fuels, carbon dioxide is formed (instead of carbon monoxide or carbon) together with water.

Compound – a substance formed when the atoms of different elements bond together.

Condensation – when a gas changes to a liquid.

Condensation point – the temperature at which a gas changes into a liquid.

Condensation polymer – a large molecule formed when monomers join together and small molecules are ejected.

Control variable – the variables in an experiment that should be kept the same to ensure a fair test.

Coolant – a substance that removes heat energy from other substances to prevent their temperature rising too much. Water is used as a coolant in the blast furnace to prevent the furnace from melting.

Covalent bond – a shared pair of electrons between two atoms.

Cracking – the breaking down of larger hydrocarbon molecules into smaller, more useful hydrocarbon molecules. This is usually done using heat and a catalyst.

Crystallisation – the formation of solute crystals when a highly concentrated solution is cooled down following evaporation.

Dependent variable – the variable that is measured for each and every change of the independent variable.

Diffusion – when particles spread out and mix. During diffusion, particles move randomly, by colliding with each other, from a region of high concentration to a region of low concentration so that they become evenly mixed.

Displacement reaction – a reaction where a more reactive element replaces a less reactive element from its compound.

Distillation – the process of separating a liquid from dissolved solids, so it separates a solvent from its solution. The solution is heated until the solvent boils, turns into a vapour and is condensed back to a pure liquid in a condenser. See also fractional distillation.

Electrode – the conducting material that dips into the electrolyte in an electrolysis cell. This is often made of carbon (graphite).

Electrolysis – the breakdown of an ionic compound molten or in aqueous solution by the passage of electricity.

Electrolysis cell – the apparatus in which electrolysis takes place, consisting of the electrolyte in a container and two electrodes connected to a dc power supply.

Electrolyte – the substance that conducts electricity and is broken down by it during electrolysis.

Electron – a sub-atomic particle found in shells around the nucleus of an atom. It has a relative mass of $\frac{1}{1840}$ and a relative charge of –1.

Electronic structure (electronic configuration) – the arrangement of electrons in shells for a particular atom.

Element – a substance made up of only one type of atom. Elements cannot be broken down into anything simpler by chemical means.

Empirical formula – the simplest whole number ratio of the atoms of each element in a compound.

Endothermic reaction – a reaction in which energy is taken in from the surroundings as reactants form products. The temperature of the surroundings falls.

Enzyme – a biological catalyst, produced by living cells to increase the rate of a reaction.

Equilibrium – when the rate of the forward reaction equals the rate of the reverse reaction for a reversible reaction in a closed container.

Evaporation – occurs below the boiling point, when some particles in a liquid have enough energy to escape from the liquid surface to form a gas.

Exothermic reaction – a reaction in which energy is given out as reactants form products. The temperature of the surroundings rises.

Fertiliser – a substance added to soil to replace nutrients lost by natural processes.

Filtration – the separation of insoluble solids from a liquid. This is often carried out in the lab using a funnel and filter paper.

Formula (plural formulae) – the use of element symbols to show how many atoms of each element are in a molecule or a formula unit of ionic compounds.

Fossil fuel – a substance formed over millions of years from the remains of dead animals and plants. Coal, natural gas and petroleum are all fossil fuels.

Fraction – this term usually applies to the fractional distillation of petroleum. A fraction is a collection of hydrocarbon compounds that have similar boiling points, so distil off at a similar position in the fractionating column.

Fractional distillation – the process of separating a liquid from a mixture of two or more liquids that have different boiling points.

Freezing – when a liquid changes to a solid.

Freezing point – the temperature at which a liquid changes to a solid.

Fuel – a substance that releases heat energy when it combusts (burns) in oxygen. This energy can be used to do work, such as generate electricity or move a car.

Fuel cell – a cell that produces electricity directly and efficiently from a chemical reaction.

Functional group – the atom, or group of atoms, responsible for the characteristic reactions of a molecule.

Galvanising – the process of coating iron with a layer of zinc to prevent rusting. The zinc provides a protective coating but, if this is scratched, the zinc (being more reactive than iron) will corrode first.

Giant covalent structure – a regular lattice where many atoms are held together by strong covalent bonds. It is called 'giant' because the arrangement is repeated many times, with large numbers of atoms bonded together.

Giant ionic structure – a regular lattice of alternating positive and negative ions. It is called 'giant' because the arrangement is repeated many times, with large numbers of ions bonded together.

Greenhouse gases – gases in the atmosphere that trap heat radiated from Earth (after it has been warmed by the Sun), causing the atmosphere to warm up.

Group – a column of the Periodic Table that contains elements with similar chemical properties. The atoms of all elements in a group have the same number of electrons in their outer shell.

Haber process – the name given to the manufacture of ammonia from nitrogen and hydrogen in the presence of an iron catalyst.

Halogen – an element in Group VII of the Periodic Table.

Glossary

Homologous series – a family of similar compounds, with similar chemical properties, due to the presence of the same functional group. The compounds in a homologous series have the same general formula and each member differs from the next by a CH_2 group. There is a gradual change in physical properties as the number of carbon atoms increases.

Hydrocarbon – a molecule containing carbon and hydrogen atoms only.

Hydrolysis – the process of breaking down a compound using water. A catalyst is often required.

Incomplete combustion – occurs when there is not enough oxygen to completely burn a compound, such as a fuel. During incomplete combustion of hydrocarbon fuels, carbon monoxide is formed and sometimes carbon, together with water.

Independent variable – the variable for which values are chosen by the investigator.

Insulator – a material, such as ceramic or plastic, that does not conduct electricity.

Ionic bond – the strong electrostatic attraction between oppositely charged ions.

Ionic compound – a compound formed when metal atoms and non-metal atoms transfer electrons to form positive and negative ions that are held together by strong electrostatic forces of attraction. It has giant ionic structure.

Ionic half-equation – the equation for the reaction that occurs at an electrode. It is balanced by using electrons, shown as e⁻.

Isotopes – atoms of the same element with the same proton number but a different nucleon number due to the different number of neutrons present. Isotopes can be radioactive or non-radioactive.

Kinetic theory or kinetic particle model of matter – the theory that explains the arrangement of particles and their motion in solids, liquids and gases. It also explains what happens during changes of state.

Lattice – a regular, three-dimensional arrangement of particles in a solid. These particles can be atoms, ions, or molecules.

Limiting reactant – the chemical that is completely used up in a reaction.

Locating agent – a chemical that makes colourless spots visible on a chromatogram.

Malleable – a property of metals, which means they can be bent and hammered into shape.

Mass number (nucleon number) – the total number of protons and neutrons in the nucleus of an atom.

Melting – when a solid changes to a liquid.

Melting point – the temperature at which a solid changes to a liquid. A pure substance has a sharp melting point.

Metallic bonding – the electrostatic force of attraction between positive metal ions and a sea of delocalised electrons.

Mixture – two or more substances that are mixed but not chemically joined together, so they can usually be separated easily.

Model – used by scientists to explain observations.

Molar gas volume – the volume occupied by one mole of any gas. At room temperature and pressure (r.t.p.), this is $24\,dm^3$ ($24\,000\,cm^3$).

Mole – the amount of substance that contains as many particles as there are atoms in exactly 12 g of carbon-12. One mole of atoms of an element is the relative atomic mass in grams. One mole of molecules of a compound is the relative molecular (or formula) mass in grams. The number of particles (atoms, molecules or formula units) in one mole is 6×10^{23}. This number is huge and is known as the Avogadro constant.

Molecular formula – the number of atoms of each element that are bonded in a molecule.

Mole ratio – the number of moles of reactants and products in a balanced equation.

Negative ions – usually formed when non-metal atoms gain electrons and become negatively charged.

Neutralisation – a reaction between an acid and a base, or alkali, to form a salt and water.

Neutral oxide – an oxide that does not react with acids or bases.

Neutron – a sub-atomic particle found in the nucleus of an atom. It has a relative mass of 1 and a relative charge of zero.

Noble gas – an element in Group VIII (or Group 0). It has a full outer shell of electrons, which makes it very stable.

Noble gas configuration (noble gas electronic structure) – when an atom, or an ion, has a full outer shell of electrons, which is a stable electron arrangement.

Non-biodegradable – used to describe a substance that cannot be broken down by microorganisms.

Non-radioactive isotopes – atoms of the same element, with stable nuclei, which do not decay or emit radiation.

Nucleon number (mass number) – the total number of protons and neutrons in the nucleus of an atom.

Glossary

Nucleus – found at the centre of the atom. The nucleus usually contains protons and neutrons. The only exception is the hydrogen atom, which has a nucleus that only contains one proton.

Ore – a rock containing a high proportion of metal or metal compound.

Oxidation – the addition of oxygen to an element or compound; the loss of electrons by a species; the increase in oxidation number of an element.

Oxidation state – a number given to an element to show how many electrons it has gained or lost. The oxidation state of a monatomic ion is the charge on that ion. When elements have more than one oxidation state in their compounds, the oxidation state is shown by a Roman numeral, e.g. iron(III) chloride shows that iron as an oxidation state of +3 in this compound.

Oxidising agent – the species that oxidises another species in a reaction and is reduced by it.

Percentage yield – used to compare the actual yield to the predicted yield in a reaction.

$$\text{percentage yield} = \frac{\text{actual yield}}{\text{predicted yield}} \times 100$$

Periods – the rows in the Periodic Table.

pH scale – a scale of numbers from 0 to 14 that measures how strong, or weak, acids and alkalis are. A neutral solution has a pH of exactly 7.

Photochemical reaction – a reaction that requires energy from light for it to occur.

Photosynthesis – the process by which plants use the energy from sunlight to react carbon dioxide and water together to make carbon-containing compounds and oxygen.

Polymer – a large molecule built up from small units called monomers.

Positive ions – usually formed when metal atoms lose electrons and become positively charged.

Predicted yield – the maximum amount of a substance that is expected to be obtained if all the reactants are converted to products. This is calculated using the chemical equation.

Product – a substance that is produced in a reaction.

Proton – a sub-atomic particle found in the nucleus of an atom. It has a relative mass of 1 and a relative charge of +1.

Proton number (atomic number) – the number of protons in the nucleus of an atom.

Radioactive isotopes – atoms of the same element, with unstable nuclei, which emit radiation and decay into different atoms. They are used in medicine to sterilise equipment and to treat cancer tumours. They are used in industry to detect leaks in pipes.

Rate of reaction – a measure of how fast a reaction goes in a given period of time.

Raw material – the starting substances in an industrial process to manufacture a chemical.

Reactant – a substance that is chemically changed when it takes part in a reaction.

Reaction – when atoms from reactants are rearranged to form new substances in the products.

Reactivity series – a list of metals placed in order of reactivity, with the most reactive metals, such as potassium, at the top. The more reactive a metal, the more easily it forms compounds in reactions and the harder it is to break these compounds down. Metals at the top of the reactivity series form positive ions much more easily than those at the bottom.

Redox reaction – a reaction in which **red**uction and **ox**idation take place.

Reducing agent – the species that reduces another species in a reaction and is oxidised by it.

Reduction – the loss of oxygen from a compound; the gain of electrons by a species; the decrease in oxidation number of an element.

Relative atomic mass, A_r – the average mass of naturally occurring atoms of an element on a scale where the ^{12}C atom has exactly 12 units.

Relative formula mass, M_r – the sum of the relative atomic masses of every atom in a formula unit of a substance. This term is usually used for ionic compounds.

Relative molecular mass, M_r – the sum of the relative atomic masses of every atom in a molecule.

Renewable fuel – a fuel made from a source that can quickly replenished (renew) itself. Wood from trees is an example of a renewable fuel and so is ethanol, if it is obtained by fermentation of plant material.

Respiration – the process by which glucose, in living cells, is converted to carbon dioxide and water with the production of energy.

Retention factor, R_f – used in chromatography.

$$R_f = \frac{\text{distance moved by substance from the baseline}}{\text{distance moved by solvent from the baseline}}$$

The R_f value for a particular substance in a particular solvent is always the same, which means that components can be identified.

Sacrificial protection – putting a metal (usually iron) in contact with a more reactive metal so that the more reactive metal corrodes first.

Salts – metal compounds formed when an acid reacts with a metal, or a base, or a carbonate.

Saturated hydrocarbon – a molecule made up of carbon atoms and hydrogen atoms only, where all the carbon atoms are joined by single bonds. Alkanes are saturated hydrocarbons.

Sea of delocalised electrons – electrons that are not associated with one particular atom and are free to move and conduct electricity. This is found in graphite and in metallic bonding.

Shells – where the electrons are arranged in an atom. Shell 1 is the closest shell to the nucleus and contains up to 2 electrons. Shell 2 contains up to 8 electrons.

Solute – the substance that is dissolved in a liquid (the solvent) to form a solution.

Solvent – the liquid that dissolves a substance (solute).

Spectator ion – an ion that does not take part in a reaction. It appears on both sides of an ionic equation.

States of matter – substances can exist as solids, liquids or gases. These are the three states of matter.

State symbols – used in equations to show whether a substance is a solid (s), liquid (l), gas (g), or is dissolved in aqueous solution (aq).

Strong acid – an acid that is fully ionised in water (aqueous solution).

Strong base – a base that is fully ionised in water (aqueous solution).

structural isomers – molecules with the same molecular formula but different structural formulae.

Sublimation – when a solid changes directly to a gas, without going through a liquid state, or when a gas changes directly to a solid, without going through a liquid state.

Sublimation point – the temperature at which a solid changes directly to a gas or a gas changes directly to a solid, without passing through a liquid state.

Substitution reaction – a reaction in which one atom, or group of atoms, is swapped for another atom, or group of atoms, in a molecule.

Thermal decomposition – the breaking down of a compound into simpler substances by heat.

Transition elements – a block of metals between Groups II and III of the Periodic Table. They are a collection of metals with high densities and high melting points. They form coloured compounds. The elements and their compounds often act as catalysts.

Unsaturated hydrocarbon – a molecule made up of carbon and hydrogen atoms only, which contains a C=C double bond. Alkenes are unsaturated hydrocarbons.

Weak acid – an acid that does not fully ionise in aqueous solutions; it only partly ionises.

Weak base – a base that does not fully ionise in aqueous solutions; it only partly ionises.

Word equation – an equation that uses the names of chemicals to show what happens in a reaction.

Yield – the mass or amount of product produced in a reaction.